Men Who Teach Young Children

IOEPress Trentham Books

Men Who Teach Young Children

An international perspective

David L. Brody

A Trentham Book
Institute of Education Press

First published in 2014 by the Institute of Education, University of London, 20 Bedford Way, London WC1H 0AL

ioepress.co.uk

British Library Cataloguing in Publication Data:
A catalogue record for this publication is available from the British Library

ISBNs
978-1-85856-517-0 (paperback)
978-1-85856-634-4 (PDF eBook)
978-1-85856-635-1 (ePub eBook)
978-1-85856-636-8 (Kindle eBook)

Typeset by Quadrant Infotech (India) Pvt Ltd
Printed by CPI Group (UK) Ltd, Croydon, CR0 4YY

Cover image: ©iStock.com/lostinbids

Contents

Acknowledgements

Writing my first book was a task that I set out to do alone, unlike other scholarly activities I have undertaken, which I have usually found partners to share the work with. I quickly discovered that this endeavour required a multitude of colleagues along every step of the way. I would like to mention them by name, and to thank them for the various kinds of help and collaboration that they afforded me.

Firstly, I am deeply indebted to the six men whose stories fill these pages. They not only opened their nurseries and classrooms, giving me free range to observe and ask questions, but they also sat with me for many hours sharing their narratives. For the ensuing months, they read their interview transcripts, answered my endless questions, and read and reread the many drafts of the chapter I wrote about them. Acting on their advice and suggested revisions was labour-intensive and enabled me to get the story right. I feel fortunate to have made their acquaintance and to have told their stories.

Similarly, I am grateful to the supervisors of these outstanding educators from around the world, who also readily agreed to be interviewed, and gave me feedback about the written material relating to them. Their contributions were invaluable in terms of rounding out my knowledge of the local context for each of the cases. These supervisors include Denise Gorthy, Eva van Oost, Eric Odenheimer, Ziona ben Hemo, Oivind Hornslien, Hana Kovler and Lorraine Khelfi. In addition, I owe special thanks to Lea Karger, a co-worker of Benny Haidlauf, who helped translate during my interview with Benny and read and commented on the drafts of parts of his chapter.

Beyond the classroom context, I found scholars and practitioners who were eager to speak to me about their own research and activities related to gender balance in early childhood education and care (ECEC) in their own country. Like those above, they provided invaluable information about the cultural contexts, and read and edited the sections of my book related to them. These collaborators include Will Parnell from the United States; Louis Tavecchio and Laut Woltring from the Netherlands; Wiebke Tennhoff, Urs Urech, Ron Halbright and Lu Decurtins from Switzerland; Anders Menka-Eide from Norway; and Julian Grenier from the UK.

In order to make sure that I accurately captured the local culture as it relates to gender balance, I asked colleagues in various countries to read my chapters and comment. Their feedback afforded thoughtful perspectives on the material. These colleagues include Diny van der Aalsvoort and Paulien

Meijer from the Netherlands, Eva Purschy from Switzerland and Kari Emilsen from Norway.

I owe special thanks to my research colleague, Linor Hadar, who provided useful feedback on the methods chapter of the book. My sister, Gayle Brody, read and edited each chapter as I completed it. Her keen reading of the manuscript helped me pick up dropped words, correct typos, and make the correct lexical choice to fit the context. I benefited from her incessant question: 'What did you mean to say here?'

Special acknowledgement and thanks go to my loving wife, Lynne Genser, both for her dedication and support, and for her tolerance and encouragement to travel to five countries to collect the data. She read every word I wrote, showing no pity in her insightful comments that demanded clarity of expression throughout the chapters. In addition, she served as a crucial sounding board for my ideas as they developed through the research and gave useful advice about solving the endless problems that arose, both on a technical and a scholarly level.

I especially wish to thank my editor, Gillian Klein, who is responsible for the publication of this book. Her unfading interest and support throughout the project has kept me going, no matter what the difficulties. Her close reading of the text and the ensuing written comments resulted in days of labour in front of the computer and, of course, a much improved manuscript. She enabled me to write what I wanted to say both clearly and concisely, to my readers' benefit. In addition, Jonathan Dore, the production editor from IOE Press, has answered every query with an unexpected politeness that always put a smile on my face.

This book is dedicated to my parents, Billye and Barney Brody, both ardent feminists, who taught me to think out of the box and to appreciate human potential regardless of gender. Their quiet inspiration enabled me to find my own path, a career dedicated to the education and care of young children, and their appreciation and celebration of cultural differences sparked the idea for this book.

Finally, I wish to acknowledge the human understanding bequeathed to me by my Maker, Creator of the Universe, who has enabled me to discover the wealth of human kindness and caring through the stories of the remarkable men I describe in this book.

David Brody
Efrat, Israel
June 2013

Foreword

The issue of men's participation in caretaking and education of the youngest is not new. Although care for small children is still widely perceived as 'women's work', there have been debates on the role of men in child-rearing for a long time. Froebel, one of the founders of the institution 'kindergarten' in the 19th century in Germany, argued that both sexes are important for the education of small children. He is cited with the words: 'Education as formation of mankind should not only be assigned to the female sex. Following the order of polarity, the male sex, teaching more from the outside, should be part of it as well'.[1] But Froebel did not succeed with his wish for male teachers – basically, because he did not find men who wanted to work in his kindergartens. Instead, women took up the new profession, and the narrative of kindergarten as 'women's work' began.

Decades later the Italian feminist Elena Belotti[2] asked in her classic book on girls' socialization: 'why should we not propose that men work as educators?' Whereas in Froebel's understanding men and women represented polar opposites, Belotti hoped for the contrary: 'The presence of women and men in kindergartens and pre-schools would give children an impression of effective reciprocity, and this would automatically work against the polarization of gender-specific roles'.[3]

At the same time, the American Kelvin Seifert published several articles, which sound surprisingly contemporary: 'Almost unanimously, leaders in the field have concluded that early childhood education needs more men. Some feel that having men will facilitate sex-role identification, especially for the boys ... But others argue the opposite: they say that including men will help to show children that sex roles are not necessary ... Either way, paradoxically, it is believed that the children will benefit. Why, then, have more men not appeared?'.[4]

These considerations, written many decades ago, reflect ambiguities and contradictions still persisting in debates on men in early childhood education today. What has happened since? In the last 15 years there has been a growing interest in the issue worldwide. Surveys have shown that parents want more male teachers, also in pre-school. In several countries, there has been public support and governmental funding for initiatives and projects towards more men in the field. International organizations see a more gender-balanced workforce as crucial for the further development of the sector. The OECD report, Starting Strong II, recommended that 'strategies are needed to recruit and retain a well-qualified, diverse, mixed-gender workforce'.[5] And in 2011, the European Commission stated that gender balance among Early Childhood Education and Care (ECEC) staff is 'a very important issue', and concluded: 'There is a pressing need to make a career in the ECEC sector more attractive to men in all EU countries'.[6] So it seems that the issue has arrived on the political agenda at least in some parts of the world. At the same time, male workers themselves have formed networks and support groups in many countries. National conferences are held, and websites document debates and activities.

There is also growing research interest. Two decades ago the issue was nearly non-existent in international research. At a conference of the European Early Childhood Education Research Association (EECERA) in 2013, results from 12 research projects on men and gender balance in the ECEC workforce were presented, covering different areas of research and a wide range of countries, including Turkey and China. Experts from 15 countries have formed an international research network, building on networks established in the 1990s. It can be concluded that gender balance in the ECEC workforce now has become an international issue.

But do we see results of these activities? In some countries, the number of male workers in ECEC has more than doubled in the last 15 years, e.g. Germany, Norway and Turkey. Still, the proportion of male workers remains low worldwide, as the expansion of institutional care for children has resulted in a huge increase of employment in many countries. The vast majority of workers is still female. Even in Norway, where several action plans included measures for more male workers, only 10 per cent of kindergarten workers are male, falling far short of the 20 per cent goal set in 1997. In most countries, less than 3 per cent of ECEC workers are men. ECEC is still 'a woman's world', in which men are always visible as 'others' – sometimes welcomed and idealized, sometimes looked at with skepticism and distrust. A closer look reveals that despite the positive attitudes towards more men in ECEC that are expressed in public surveys or in statements of politicians, initiatives for a more gender-balanced workforce strongly depend on the devoted work of engaged individuals. To name but a few, Bryan Nelson in the USA, Kenny Spence in Scotland, Jan Peeters in Belgium, Sarah Farquhar in New Zealand, and, recently, Bernhard Koch in Austria, have promoted projects and supported men working in the field for many years now.

David Brody, the author of this book, stands among these leaders. David is not only an experienced teacher and researcher, but he is also a man who is able to listen in a way that helps people open up their mind and express what is really important for them. With his background as a male

ECEC worker, as well as an immigrant from the USA to Israel, he is the right person to conduct the cross-cultural research on men presented in this book.

When I was introduced to the work of David and his colleagues Yael Dayan and Yair Perez, I was impressed by their efforts to form a support group for male ECEC students and workers in Israel. David and his colleagues conducted interviews with several members of the group, revealing profound insights into how they experienced their situation as men working with children, often as the only man in their institution. It is striking how similar their experiences were to those I have heard in many years of counselling groups of male ECEC workers in Germany.

While I was conducting a research project in Austria, including a full survey of all male workers and students in ECEC, David travelled around the world to investigate not only the personal stories of experienced male ECEC workers, but also the socio-cultural contexts of their countries. Again, there were many similarities. Despite all cultural differences, men working with children seem to have much in common all over the world. As David points out in this book, he 'continued to be amazed at similarities between the men, even in the way they expressed ideas, and in their viewpoints'. This notion is supported by an international overview showing similar issues arising in most countries, even in countries with very different gender cultures and ECEC systems, e.g. the Nordic countries, Switzerland, Turkey, New Zealand, or even China.[7]

On the other hand, differences between cultures and systems are evident. For example, the Nordic countries have a long history of gender equality, and governments have supported male involvement in the family for decades. In other countries, traditional gender roles are still widely accepted, and the responsibility of women for child-rearing has not been questioned. In some countries early childhood education is a part of the public educational system, while in others care for children mostly remains in the private sector. Also, systems of vocational training and the level of academization are very diverse. But at first sight, statistical data do not reveal how all these differences contribute to differences in male participation in the ECEC workforce.

So what is universal? What makes a difference? These are questions of cross-cultural research in general, and also the main questions of this book. With a broad array of questions, David visited six experienced male ECEC workers from different countries in their work environment. He observed them in their everyday life and interactions, and listened to them in lengthy interviews. The case studies offer fascinating insights into the lives of men devoted to work with small children. David dives into their world to understand the motives and philosophy of these men, always with a positive approach that highlights the personal competencies and strengths of these men. Moreover, he seeks to understand how these men construct their masculinity, and how aspects of gender roles influence their professional development and self-identity. In addition, the author thoroughly researched the societal contexts of the six countries. Gender roles and gender equality, as well as attitudes and measures regarding men in ECEC, are reviewed and discussed with experts from each country.

The comparison of the six cases opens up new perspectives, highlighting both the variety and the commonalities among men from different societies. The comparison reveals how institutional contexts as well as cultural norms and attitudes regarding men as caregivers affect the professional lives of individual men working with children. The book's findings clearly point to the importance of the diversity of masculinities of the portrayed men, matched with their respect for and interest in children, for shaping their contribution to caring and education of young children. The men in the study express their masculinity in different ways, but they also cross boundaries of gendered dispositions. The findings suggest a new definition of professionalism in ECEC built on the voices and the experiences of men working in the field.

Finally, I must mention the deep empathy that is characteristic of David's approach to his interview partners. This becomes especially apparent when it comes to the issue of the isolation of the male childcare worker, e.g. when one of the interviewees expresses his wish to meet other men who work in this field. In many years of working with groups of men in ECEC, I have often experienced how important it can be for these men to meet other men engaged in their field.

This voice of the isolated childcare worker or teacher reaching out for collegiality was what touched me most when I heard of the grassroots support group David and his colleagues have established in Israel. The experience of the mutual support among men from different worlds enabled these men to overcome their differences and conflicts that shape Israel's society today. As one member of the group explained: 'One of the most exciting things about it was meeting Israeli men, and see the range of characters: religious educators, orthodox men, and settlers, and others who are secular from Tel-Aviv, leftist, and from all walks of life. And we all came because of our passion for education, through action, wanting to share, perhaps to become more professional and feel part of a group. I think it is very, very important'.[8]

Giving men the opportunity to express themselves, as well as to listen to others, despite disparities and boundaries set up by gender, race, religion, political attitudes or institutional backgrounds, forms the core for our engagement for more men in ECEC. The inclusion of more men can contribute to the development of early childhood institutions as places for well-being and good development of children, parents, workers, and the society as a whole.

It is this devotion to make the world a better place, for children as well as for all men and women, that drives the work of those interested in gender balance in ECEC. By sharing stories from male workers from around the world, this book opens up new perspectives for understanding and dialogue. Enjoy reading!

Tim Rohrmann

Dr Tim Rohrmann, Psychologist, is one of the leading experts for gender issues in Early Childhood Education in Germany. Currently working at Evangelic High School, Dresden, Germany, he is founder and co-convenor of the EECERA Special Interest Group 'Gender Balance', an international research network on men and gender in ECEC.

Notes

[1] Rabe-Kleberg, U. (2003) *Gender Mainstreaming und Kindergarten* [Gender Mainstreaming and Kindergarten]. Weinheim: Beltz, 44. German, translation TR.

[2] Belotti, E. (1973) *Dalla parte delle bambine*. Milan: Feltrinelli. [Published in German (1975) *Was geschieht mit den kleinen Mädchen?* Munich: Frauenoffensive; and in English (1976) *What Are Little Girls Made Of? The roots of feminine stereotypes*. New York: Schocken Books.]

[3] Belotti, E. (1973) *Dalla parte delle bambine*. Milan: Feltrinelli. [Published in German (1975) *Was geschieht mit den kleinen Mädchen?* Munich: Frauenoffensive; and in English (1976) *What Are Little Girls Made Of? The roots of feminine stereotypes*. New York: Schocken Books, 23, translation TR.]

[4] Seifert, K. (1974) 'Getting men to teach preschool'. *Contemporary Education*, 45 (4), 299–302, 299; see also Seifert, K. (1973) 'Some problems of men in childcare work'. *Child Welfare*, 52 (3), 167–71.

[5] OECD (2006) *Starting Strong II. Early childhood education and care policy*. Paris: OECD, 158.

[6] European Commission (2011) *Early Childhood Education and Care: Providing all our children with the best start for the world of tomorrow*. Brussels: Communication of the Commission, 17.2.2011. Online. http://ec.europa.eu/education/school-education/doc/childhoodcom_en.pdf , 8 (accessed September 2013).

[7] Rohrmann, T. (2012) 'Maenner in der Elementarpaedagogik: Ein aktueller internationaler Ueberblick' ['Men in ECE: An updated international overview']. In M. Cremers, S. Hoeyng, J. Krabel and T. Rohrmann (eds). *Maenner in Kitas* [Men in ECE institutions], 289–306. Opladen: Barbara Budrich. (German).

[8] Dayan, Y., Perez, Y. and Brody, D.L. (2013) 'A grassroots support group for male early childhood educators: Implications for practice'. Presentation on the 23rd EECERA Annual Conference, Tallinn, Estonia, August.

Chapter 1
Knocking at the door

My first brush with failure and success in landing a job with young children took place in the spring of 1972 in Israel. Searching for a kindergarten teaching position led me to the Jerusalem office of the state inspector, who responded to my request to teach 5-year-olds with derisive laughter. Undiscouraged by this rejection, I turned to the central office of one of the kibbutz organizations and was immediately referred to a kibbutz on the northern border of the country. I was quickly invited for an interview, and was pleasantly surprised at the enthusiastic greeting I received at the hands of a committee of parents and educators, who showed me around the small village, spoke to me about my educational philosophy and hired me on the spot.

My life's circumstances did not permit me to take the job; however, this exhilarating event bolstered my self-confidence to continue my job search a few months later when I moved halfway across the world to Cambridge, Massachusetts. There I was offered a position in the 4-year-old class at the Harvard Law School Day Care Center, where I launched my career as an early childhood educator. My own confrontations with gender bias and gender acceptance in these varied circumstances exemplify the critical influence of culture on the participation of men in the early childhood workforce. In my case, I experienced societal polar opposites. The state inspector in Jerusalem represented the conventions of a traditional urban western culture of the 1970s in which gender roles were strictly prescribed. The kibbutz parents presented a different ethos that replaced urban values with ideals meant to achieve social and gender equality through a communist micro-economy and social reorganization. Across the ocean, my success in Cambridge, Massachusetts must be viewed in the historical context of the American social upheavals of the 1960s, in which racial justice, feminism and anti-war rhetoric were central to cultural fermentation. This focus on social contexts and their influence on the life of one young man seeking to work with preschoolers at a particular time in different cultural settings serves to frame the broader question of how culture and society influence the inclusion of men in the early childhood workforce, and is the topic of my book.

Men have been choosing to work with young children in public and private institutions for decades, although their numbers are few. The normative reaction to this career choice ranges from surprise and tolerance to derision and suspicion. Nowadays, there are many cases of men who are enjoying legitimate employment as caregivers in nurseries and kindergarten classes in nations around the world. Their status as Early Childhood Education and Care (ECEC)[1] workers is coming to be recognized as gender appropriate not only by the institutions in which they work, but also by their family and friends and by the parents of the children they teach. Beyond this tolerant acceptance, there is growing recognition of the unique contribution of men to the education of young children and a claim that this valuable human resource should be encouraged in the ECEC workforce.

Evidence of the growing acceptance of men in ECEC can be found in the call by the Childcare Network of the European Commission in 1995 for member states to achieve the goal of a 20 per cent male early childhood workforce (Peeters, 2013), and this concern for gender balance was once again voiced a decade later in an OECD report on early childhood education (OECD, 2006). State-funded projects to increase the participation of men have been established in Germany, Austria, Switzerland, the UK, Belgium and Norway (Cremers, Höyng, Krabel and Rohrmann, 2012; Koch, 2012; NWSB website; Rolfe, 2005; Peeters, 2003; Johannesen and Hoel, 2010). Countries outside the EU such as New Zealand and even China have stepped forward with initiatives to promote the inclusion of men in the ECEC workforce (Farquhar, 2008; Wu, 2010). Although no official steps have been taken in Turkey, the number of men in ECEC has been increasing there over the years (Anliak and Şahin Beyazkurk, 2008). In the United States interest has also been expressed in increasing the number of men as caregivers and preschool teachers. For example, the premier American organization for early childhood education, the National Association for the Education of Young Children (NAEYC), dedicated a special issue of its professional journal, *Young Children*, in 2002 to the importance of men in the field, and several articles on the topic have appeared later (Friedman, 2010; Eisenhauer and Pratt, 2010).

The positive trend in public opinion regarding the value of men as caregivers and teachers of young children and the increasingly positive attitudes of administrators and policymakers towards achieving gender balance must be viewed realistically against a less favourable backdrop. Men 'continue to experience bias in the hiring process; inequitable workloads, salaries and resources; and limited opportunities for growth' (Watson and Woods, 2011: xv). Much research has focused on the question of why so few men enter the profession. Nelson (2002) conducted a national survey among NAEYC members which pointed to three primary reasons for men's reluctance to teach young children: stereotypes (women's work, men are not nurturers, homophobia), fear of abuse allegations and the low status of the profession.

In his review of the literature, Peeters (2013) concurred with Nelson (2002) that a primary block to men entering ECEC is the widespread perception that childcare is women's work. He cites evidence that female professions are not attractive to men and that gender segregation perpetuates itself. He adds that men in ECEC carry with them the constant fear of being accused of paedophilia, a feeling that results in vigilance regarding their physical contact with children. Add to this the low status of childcare work (Rolfe, 2005) and it is no wonder that men are reluctant to choose work with young children as a lifelong calling. Thus the trend towards positive inclusion of men in the profession continues to be challenged by stereotyped attitudes that compete with the more liberal views which have begun to percolate upwards in the gender balance discourse among parents, administrators and other stakeholders.

A cross-cultural view on the experiences and contributions of men in ECEC has yet to be conducted. Although several studies have looked at men in a single culture, no research has been found that compares this phenomenon between societies. Our understanding of the effects of culture on the many aspects of gender balance is therefore limited to the perspectives of researchers within their own country. In addition, the existing studies look at different aspects of the issue, making comparison problematic. I conceived my research design to address this gap in scholarship on gender balance from a cross-cultural perspective. Specifically I have chosen to focus on the experiences of men prior to and during their employment as caregivers and teachers of young children. By looking closely at several cases in different cultures, I seek to understand better the commonalities and the uniqueness of men who have sought the ECEC profession from their own social perspective.

In this book I examine the issues that men face when they choose to work with young children. In the countries I have studied, I have found an almost universal norm that teaching young children is women's work. Thus the starting point for the men in this study is the same: they all chose to cross the gender boundary. The nature of this boundary, their ease or difficulty in crossing it, and the experiences they encountered on the job, vary greatly according to the different socio-cultural contexts. The theoretical framing for my study focuses on issues relevant to men's entry into and participation in ECEC, including the notions of role model, caring, physical contact with children, and dilemmas related to men's gender identity. Ideally I would present each of these issues from a multicultural perspective, showing how each of the social contexts of my study treats these topics. To my disappointment, I learned that anthropological research around these themes either has not been conducted or is not accessible to the English-speaking researcher. In the light of this limitation, I present in this chapter theoretical material and research findings on these topics based on the monocultures in which the studies were conducted. I lay out the groundwork here for the six case studies that comprise the main corpus of the book. As the first of its kind, this pioneering study will hopefully lead to further cross-cultural research in the future.

Gender balance discourses

The discussions surrounding men in ECEC was brought into focus by Nordberg (2004) in a paper she presented at a Scandinavian conference on women and men in the Nordic labour market. She identified ten themes found in discourses on gender balance among early childhood professionals and scholars. These discourses emerge from the background of hegemonic masculinity that places men in dominant roles and women in subordinate functions (Connell, 2005). Male hegemony is not only taken for granted in the early childhood setting, but also regulates the behaviour of both men and women who work there. Among Nordberg's paradigms are discourses related to the male role model, the new man, the fear of femininity and effeminate men, the nature of gender equality and the undermining of the gender dichotomy.

The discourses identified by Nordberg not only address policy issues regarding the need to attract more men to work with young children but also reveal a more personal stratum as well as issues related to men's unique contribution to ECEC, an inquiry deeply embedded in the discourse on masculinity. The notion that men have something special to offer in the care and education of young children is tied to the question of what early childhood education has to offer to men. So we need to consider how working with young children both enhances and challenges the personal and professional identities of the men who choose this work.

Men's lives documented

Two important collections of men's narratives have been published in the past 15 years, each with a different analytical focus. The stories in these compendia reveal the personal journeys of men who chose to work with young children, and describe in their own words these individuals' entry into the profession as well as their practice. In his book, *Uncommon Caring*, James King presents brief narratives of six men who teach from kindergarten to grade 3 (1998).[2] He frames these chapters with a close examination of the concept of *caring*, as formulated by Noddings (2003, 2005) in her pioneering study of how women differ from men in their interactions with those they encounter in their work. Drawing on these written narrative interviews and focus-group discussions, King concludes that caring takes on different forms for these men than for women in the profession. For example, touch is viewed as an important aspect of caring. Because physical contact with children can be problematic, men have developed alternative modes of caring, such as active listening. Sargent (2004) calls these 'compensatory activities' that 'engage children in learning in the absence of nurturing' (ibid.: 185). In this statement Sargent equates nurturing with physical contact, to the exclusion of other types of behaviour that might also be considered to show nurturance. King also brings to the fore these men's rejection of female styles of teaching, and shows how their need to find appropriate male teaching models occupies their energies.

Employing a different approach, Lemuel Watson and Sheldon Woods invited men who work with young children to write in-depth narrative biographical essays. In *Go Where You Belong* (2011), their accounts describe the trajectories of those who remained in the classroom as well as those who moved into academic and administrative positions. The editors frame the narrative chapters with a description of these men as cultural workers who 'survive and thrive' (ibid.: xvii). In the concluding chapter, Woods expresses the aim of the book as highlighting the 'practical challenges of being a male and an early childhood or early elementary teacher in contemporary society' (155). Such challenges include the suspicions of administrators in the hiring process and those of parents in the initial days of the school year. The contributors also address problematic interactions with female colleagues. What stands out in all of the material is the unswerving commitment to quality interactions with children, a passion for teaching, and the pleasure accrued from these significant interactions.

Paul Sargent's book, entitled *Real Men or Real Teachers?* (Sargent, 2001), also addresses the tensions in the personal and professional lives of men who work with young children, showing how issues of stress relate to their career choice. Drawing on his interviews with kindergarten and elementary school teachers, Sargent identifies several critical concerns including scrutiny about touch, the gendered world of elementary school teaching, male role models for boys and girls, and the isolation of the male primary school teacher. His research unpacks the many elements that play a part in the formation of the men's personal and professional identity, and reveals for us the inherent stress in the daily work of these men.

The male role model

The discourse on the male role model as raised by Nordberg (2004) appears time and again through the literature on gender balance. One of the common arguments enlisted for increasing men in the ECEC workforce is the notion that teaching has become feminized and that male role models are lacking in the daily lives of children (Drudy, 2008). This deficit of male role models is viewed as particularly detrimental to boys and has led to a popular suggestion that gender matching between teacher and children will improve the achievement of students. This hypothesis was investigated in a qualitative study which showed that 7–8-year-olds and their teachers in England rejected the importance and necessity of gender matching between pupils and their teachers (Francis *et al.*, 2006). In a Dutch study of grade 8 pupils, no causal effect was found between the gender of the teacher and the achievement, behaviour or attitudes of the students (Driessen, 2007). Cameron (2006), in a review of the research, articulates the arguments that men in the nursery and kindergarten provide someone with whom boys can identify. In a somewhat contradictory stance, these same men are expected to show children that 'manliness can include caring' (Parkin, cited in Cameron, 2001: 436). At the time of her review in 2001, Cameron found no research supporting the claim that gender differences influence teacher effectiveness. Furthermore, she reports on research indicating that minority genders in a workforce often serve to entrench gender role stereotypes (Allan, cited in Cameron, 2001: 436). Despite this empirical evidence, the argument for increasing men in ECEC continues to gain favour among not only policymakers and administrators but also the men who work with young children.

In a more nuanced presentation of the role model discourse, Sargent (2001) found that the American men he interviewed regarded the construct of male role model as a source of stress in their professional lives. All the men in his study keenly felt the expectation that they would serve as a gendered role model, whether they wanted it or not. Interestingly, they described this function for girls in more vivid terms than for boys, an indication of their overall rejection of the importance of this function for the boys. Parents, particularly single mothers, expected them to present a role model for their sons that included being 'the man in their lives', an interest in athletics, a disciplinarian, an authority figure and a lack of interest in art and poetry. In response to these expectations, the teachers were generally uncomfortable with being asked to model such stereotypical masculine behaviour.

Touching and caring

According to Sargent (2004), the constant scrutiny that men in ECEC experience is part and parcel of their professional lives. Men must take their gender into account at all times. Unlike women, they are under constant suspicion of paedophilia, which leads them to extreme vigilance regarding physical contact with the children. One of Sargent's informants states that women's laps are a safe place and men's laps are dangerous. He generalizes that 'the act most seen as open to suspicion is having a child sit on a man's lap' (ibid.: 178). In their study of American male pre-service teachers, Cooney and Bittner (2001) used a focus-group method. When one student reported that parents had requested that he refrain from changing their child's nappy, he responded with extreme consternation. The group suggested that building trust with the children and parents was the appropriate remedy for these parental suspicions. This finding is indicative of the overarching issue of the inherent problems of touch for men in ECEC. The very essence of early childhood education is placing the emotional and social needs of the child first. By anyone's standards, young children require physical contact with their caregivers and teachers. Physical attention through hugs, lap sitting, a pat on the head and even a kiss are examples of parenting behaviour that are common among female caregivers and are viewed as natural and positive contributions to the emotional well-being of the young child. While men in ECEC are expected in many ways to provide a male role model, even replacing the absent father, they are discouraged from these parental modes of interaction. This dilemma relates back to our exploration of the male role model expectation, which has been found to be uncomfortable for many men. Certainly one aspect of this template is that the man will show little emotion, in order to demonstrate manliness. Nordberg (2004) refers to this discourse as 'the traditional man' contrasted to the 'new man' who is 'nice and emotional' but should act and look like a 'real man'. It seems that there is tremendous ambivalence about initiating physical contact for either of these extremes of masculinity. The resulting contradiction places men in what Sargent (2004) calls 'between a rock and a hard place'.

Intertwined with the issue of touch is the broader issue of caring. It is impossible to separate best practices of early childhood teaching from notions of caring. Because caring has traditionally characterized the way women interact with the world, the caring professions have long been thought of as feminine. When men enter this world, several basic assumptions are challenged. First of all, the question is asked: Are men able to do the job well? Are men capable of caring? Secondly, the identity of the men who choose this job is often called into question: Are they real men? Thirdly and most importantly, how do these men work with young children? Do they show caring, and if so, how? A plethora of studies over the past two decades have addressed these questions, and shed light on the complexities of the issue. Unfortunately, almost all of the research has been done on men who are training for positions or who teach in the primary grades (Watson and Woods, 2011; Sargent, 2001; King, 1998). Very little attention has been paid to the men who work with children ages 0–6.

The caring literature premises an inextricable bond between mothering, caring and teaching (Forrester, 2005). Historically the roots of these notions can be found in Froebel's writings about 'natural mothering and how it can be made conscious in the classroom' (Acker, 1995: 23). Gilligan (1995) provides a theoretical framework for the strong identification of women with caring. She claims that the socialization of women inducts them into a relational mode, and she contrasts this with the patriarchal paradigm that values autonomy and disconnection over the feminine concern for others. Both Gilligan and Acker agree that caring is considered to be a female trait by society because of the roles assigned to women, roles that require acts of caring. They claim that caring is not inherently biological.

Taking this analysis one step further, Acker shows how schools are set up to encourage caring between the teachers themselves and between teachers and children, as part of the task of the female teacher. Nias (1999) has even called primary teaching a 'culture of care' that includes six dimensions: 'affectivity, responsibility for learners, responsibility for the relationships in the school, self-sacrifice, over-conscientiousness and identity' (ibid.: 66). King (1998) expands on the idea that for primary teachers, a central expression of caring is commitment, which means teachers' involving their whole selves in their work, blurring the boundaries between their private and professional lives. This analysis is reminiscent of Nias' dimension of over-conscientiousness.

Caring is a central aspect of work with young children, and this commonplace seems to be so obvious that it does not warrant discussion in the research literature. Moyles (2001) raised the question about passion in the early childhood classroom, and suggests that the ECEC worker must *a priori* make a commitment that is passionate. It is precisely this unstated assumption about the necessity of caring that creates conflict and stress for the men who work with young children. They understand precisely what best practice consists of, yet they feel uncomfortable engaging in caring behaviour for a number of reasons. One source of hesitation is fear of being accused of paedophilia. As mentioned in the section on touch, men feel like their lap is off limits for children. Similarly, they avoid feminine behaviour in order to avoid assumptions that they may be gay. This dilemma relates to Nordberg's discourse on the fear of the feminine and the fear of effeminate men, which certainly occupies the thoughts of many men in ECEC. Oyler, Jennings and Lozada (2001) presented a case study of an ex-marine who chose a second career in ECEC. One of his biggest adjustment problems was understanding the language of care among his female colleagues. He simply did not relate to 'care talk' (King, 1998), preferring action-oriented language instead of 'soft and nurturing talk' (ibid.). In their research on novice men teachers in Australia, Hansen and Mulholland (2005) found that their subjects avoided touching as a form of caring and instead generated alternative gender-acceptable modes of behaviour. The first was to view touching as unprofessional. A second was to show affection through talking and listening with empathy. A third was to encourage others to touch, while the men circumscribed their own behaviour. A fourth was to use the disciplinary role, which is a safe zone for men, in a caring way. Finally, the men showed caring by establishing meaningful relationships with children and by creating community.

Men's own ideas about caring can be examined using Vogt's (2002) continuum of caring behaviour. The scale is based on findings from a study of primary school teachers in England who each described what caring meant to them. Vogt's conclusions are presented in her description of the primary school teacher's ethical orientation towards care: 'The continuum moves from caring as being committed, caring as developing relationships, caring as maintaining physical well-being, to expressing care with a cuddle, caring as parenting and caring as mothering' (ibid.: 262).

One dimension by which this continuum can be viewed is inclusiveness/exclusiveness in terms of gender role identification. While one end of the scale, mothering, is closely linked to femininity and thereby exclusive, the other end of the scale, commitment, has a less gendered identity and is more inclusive. Hansen and Mulholland's (2005) study reveals how novice men teachers tend to exhibit caring behaviour that is inclusive and has a more ambiguous gender identity, such as showing commitment and developing relationships. In Vogt's analysis of the caring continuum, no mention is made of cultural relativism. Noddings defines caring as a relational matter, as expressed between the carer and the cared for in the 'caring encounter' (2001: 99). Webb-Dempsey *et al.* (1996) recognize that caring is manifested in different ways across cultures. Thus caring behaviour that appears at different points on Vogt's continuum may be more or less emphasized by different societies.

To summarize this section on caring as a problematic area for men in ECEC, I cite Nodding's (2001) important discussion of the tension that arises between caring and professionalism in teaching. She suggests that the application of achievement standards in primary schools reduces the possibilities for teachers' caring behaviour, as teachers are increasingly being called upon to produce results such as academic achievement at the expense of pursuing social and emotional goals for their students. The central role of caring in the ECEC teacher's role definition heightens the conflict. Caring and professionalism overlap and may be considered to exist compatibly until men enter the picture. Can men be early childhood professionals who exhibit caring, or is a different standard of professionalism being applied to them than to women? This question has yet to be resolved, and it raises important issues in the discourse of men participating in the ECEC workforce.

Masculinity under the magnifying glass

The role model and caring discourses described above touch on the question of masculinity as an essential component of the personal and professional identity of men who work in ECEC. Although these men typically choose the profession because of their commitment and ideals, they find themselves from the outset circumscribed by the social norms that they have dared to challenge. A current body of research on the concept of gender intensification among adolescents sheds light on gender identity and choice of profession. Sinclair and Carlson (2013) found a strong correlation between gender identity threat and adolescents' stereotypical occupational preferences. This finding supports the argument that men with traditional and rigid gender definitions are unlikely to choose ECEC as a lifelong endeavour.

Connell (2009) describes gender as a socially constructed reality that expresses itself on four dimensions: power, production, emotion and symbol. Men who work in the nursery or kindergarten class define themselves differently for each of these dimensions. In terms of power, they relinquish the 'male hegemonic dividend' (Connell, 2005) by placing themselves in a women's profession with lower income potential (England and Herbert, 1993) and lower status. On the other hand, they also may take advantage of the 'glass escalator' (Williams, 1992), a well-known phenomenon of men rising to better-paid positions such as day care director or school manager, if they choose to leave the classroom.

In terms of production, they are considered by large parts of society to be doing women's work, having relinquished their gender privilege of male productivity. The emotional dimension relates to the value of caring in the early childhood work context. As discussed above, this expectation is fraught with contradictions that impinge on the man's professional and personal identity, as he must resolve the dilemma of carrying out the emotional demands of his job while self-monitoring in order to protect himself (Martino and Frank, 2006). Men who work in ECEC are viewed by many as 'classic tokens' in terms of gender anomaly (Sargent, 2004). Thus their masculinity is partially defined by this symbolic stance of being seen as a stereotyped representation of others in the same situation. This means that their actions are construed as representative of all men, which places a heavy burden on them. While each of the dimensions defines men's relationship to both men and women in the society, they exist concomitantly and create a nexus of stressors for the men, who are dealing with their own masculinity on a day-to-day basis. Men in ECEC cannot take their masculinity for granted. Rather they 'must remain conscious of their gender and monitor their presentation at all times in order to present correct gender displays' (Sargent, 2004: 186).

While these dimensions of gender help us focus on specific stressors, Connell's (2005) earlier description of masculine performance suggests that men construct different masculinities, and that the relationship between these types can be defined. According to Connell, men create their masculinity through relationships with other men and in response to how other men view them. Thus the four types of relationships that exist between the various masculinities deepen our understanding of the social structures that must be negotiated when a man crosses the occupational gender boundary. *Hegemonic* masculinity is the social standard against which all other masculinities are measured. This construct includes patriarchal privilege and power over others. A gender hierarchy among men implies that there are *subordinate* masculinities, over which the hegemonic order clearly reigns. An example of a subordinate masculinity is homosexuality, which in the past has been disparaged and oppressed by the hegemonic order. Connell's definition of *complicity* as a third form of masculinity deals with the reality that very few men actually embody hegemonic masculinity to the fullest. Many men enjoy the patriarchal dividend by subscribing to hegemonic values, while at the same time sharing with their wives some traditional female roles such as housework or childcare. The fourth classification is *marginalized* masculinity, a term describing the relationship between men in the dominant and lower social classes. Thus black men in a racist society are denigrated by hegemonic white men.

The men who choose to work with young children may be thought of as representing a subordinate masculinity (Sargent, 2004). One of the challenges to these men's identities is the notion that they are not real men as defined by hegemonic standards, rather they are lesser men who have foregone hegemonic privilege by engaging in women's work. Because both homosexuals and male childcare workers have been defined as subordinate masculinities, it is important to distinguish between the two. Homosexuals have clearly rejected the male hegemonic norm of heterosexuality. Men who work with young children have rejected the divisive norm that sets men apart from women in terms of career choice. These men have embraced an egalitarian stance which says that men are suited to engage in caring activities as a profession. As such they may be looked down upon by other men, who might find such an approach threatening to their male dominance. Jones (2007) describes a binary gender paradigm in which female and male characteristics are seen as polar opposites. Following this construct, men who choose to work with young children may be understood to violate the binary nature of gender definitions, as they place themselves somewhere between the gender extremes dictated by society.

Such self-definition may also result in a subordinated masculinity, as defined by Connell. Connell's description of the relationships between the different masculinities may also be applied to men in ECEC by viewing them in the category of complicity. Men in ECEC are typically pushed into asserting their masculinity in order to avoid being identified with other subordinate masculinities. They do not want to appear feminine in any way, shape or form (Nordberg, 2004). Coulter (1993) found that men were faced with extreme pressure from the female staff and the children to exhibit traditional male traits, thereby reinforcing conventional patterns of sex differentiation.

In an American study of men who teach music, traditionally a woman's role, the men were found to reinforce masculine stereotypes (Roulston and Mills, 2000). Martino and Frank (2006) found that Australian men in the lower primary grades exhibit these examples of complicity behaviour in order to maintain a clear masculine role model for the boys they teach. This complicity approach indeed reinforces stereotypically male behaviour, and may be seen as counterproductive to the establishment of a new gender order. While many argue that men in the early childhood settings can provide role models of a gentler, different kind of man, the reality has been found in many cases to fall far short of this ideal. Thus men may overemphasize certain hegemonic masculine qualities, such as playing sports, taking responsibility for technology in the school, or simply by offering heroic measures such as moving heavy furniture for their women colleagues. Whether they exhibit complicity or suffer from subordination, these men are clearly responding to the masculinity challenges that confront them in their work situation.

When viewed through the lens of Connell's paradigms of different masculinities, these studies of men in ECEC paint a rather bleak picture of how masculinity affects their professional identities. However, there is a brighter side, which is evidenced in data brought by Skelton (2003) in her interviews with British lower primary teachers (ages 3–8) and upper primary teachers (ages 7–11). The teachers of the older children were highly concerned about their masculine image, which they wanted to conform to a traditional model, but the teachers of the younger children were not. Skelton suggests that the teachers of the lower primary grades were committed to and comfortable with their career choice. Furthermore, she hypothesized that they were more comfortable with their sexuality than the group teaching older children. In this study we see the possibility of another type of masculinity, which Jones (2007) calls 'hybridized', a term that suits the postmodern man. This construct allows for multiple masculinities, according to context, and perhaps a blending of the hegemonic model with a softer, more caring face. Coulter and Greig (2008) review studies about the attitudes of men training to be elementary school teachers in Canada. They found that these student teachers revealed a liberal masculinity, in spite of pressures placed on them to exhibit traditional traits.

Most of the studies that focus on the construction of masculinity among early childhood educators deal with primary school teachers, not with those who work with preschool children. Professional literature and published descriptions of nursery and kindergarten teachers give backing to Skelton's hypothesis of increased gender self-confidence as one moves down the age range. Take, for example, Eisenhauer and Pratt's description of an American kindergarten teacher as a very caring man whose only identification with a traditional masculinity was his deep voice (2010). A second article of this genre was written by Friedman (2010) who presented brief profiles of four American men working with young children. They stress a softer, caring side with no emphasis on traditional male traits. Along with the 'new man' image (Nordberg, 2004), these men without exception enlist the male role model discourse as their *raison d'être* for working with young children, an indication that certain masculine traits are very important to them. Another such article about a Swiss teacher appeared in a popular magazine, portraying a veteran male teacher as a particularly caring individual who blended these softer aspects of his work with clear hegemonic masculine traits (Olivier, 2011). The portrayal of these men as caring teachers reveals another type of masculinity that is open to social change and potential gender equality.

Gender balance discourses revisited

The growing interest among men in participating in the ECEC workforce is an outgrowth of the worldwide movement towards gender equality. In general, the push for gender equality has accompanied the change from agrarian to post-industrial economies in many countries. While economic growth was once thought to be a powerful explanation of liberal trends in human rights, this model has failed to explain differences in gender equality in states with similar economic prosperity but very different levels of equality. In their book, *Rising Tide,* Ronald Inglehart and Pippa Norris (2003) present 30 years of data from the Gender Equality Scale. Their findings link gender equality in 61 countries to various factors such as economic growth, social indicators including quality of life measures, core beliefs in society, religion, secularization and culture. This important study points to the conclusion that culture matters, and that deeply held beliefs about the role of women can either retard or push forward a nation's gender equality agenda. This long-range study supports the notion that culture has a significant part to play in the status of gender equality in any country, and lends credence to the importance of the effects of culture on men's participation in the ECEC workforce.

The gender balance discourses on which I have focused form a conglomerate of concerns for the men who choose to work with young children, no matter where they live. For example, single-parent families are common throughout the world. With the disintegration of the traditional nuclear family, educators are concerned about the effects of absent fathers and mothers on the healthy growth and development of young children. The presence of more men in the teaching workforce is seen as a way to offset the absence of fathers at home. The imperative that men in ECEC should serve as male role models is a discourse that plays itself out across national borders. However, variations in the theme need to be examined with a cultural lens.

Caregiving has different meanings in different societies. For example, policymakers in Israel have long tolerated large groups of young children with few caregivers. The OECD has calculated a ratio of children to adults by dividing the total number of children enrolled in ECEC programmes by the total number of adults employed in those same programmes (OECD, 2012: 342–3). According to these calculations, Israel has the second highest ratio among the 31 nations included in the comparison, with a proportion of 24 children per adult. Two other countries that I studied were included in the OECD data. The ratio in Switzerland is 1:18 and in the United States 1:14. These numbers may represent an ethos of the importance of the group in the society. In Israel children are encouraged to rely on one another, as group identity has been the norm in the foundational values of this young nation. Another example of the culturally specific meaning of caregiving is the value Switzerland places on mothers staying at home to raise their children. The consequence is that most women work part-time while their children are young so they are home to care for the children after school.

While notions of care and caregiving have not been studied across societies, there are important distinctions that affect how men are viewed as caregivers, and how social expectations towards these men might differ.

Similarly, the norms of physical touch vary from culture to culture. In his classic treatise on this subject, Hall (1959) identified cultural variations and discusses how touching behaviour is proscribed or encouraged in different societies. Hofstede's comprehensive comparison of cultures, *Culture's Consequences* (2001), is a more recent and comprehensive analysis. The issue of touch for each of the men in the study was affected by its cultural dimension.

While Connell (2005) suggested that his masculinity paradigms are universal, the variations between societies are well known. For example, machismo is a classic concept of gender definition that defines how men in Latin American cultures are expected to behave (Mirande, 2010). The topic of masculinity is central to the daily lives of men who have chosen to work with young children. Keeping in mind Connell's basic structure of gender construction, I present each case within its own cultural context. As an overarching factor in identity formation, masculinity cuts across other gender balance discourses and determines the manner in which these discourses will be conducted. When considering the popularity of the discussion on the male role model, it becomes obvious that masculinity definitions determine which role model will be represented by the man who fills the role of caregiver or teacher. Likewise, the constructs of touching and caring are bound by definitions of masculinity. The limitations or licence that society places on touch and the conceptualization of caring are also determined by the models of masculinity found in that social framework. No wonder masculinity is a dominant issue when examining how men function in ECEC settings. The discourse parameters of male role model, touching and caring, and masculinity are the substrate for listening to the narratives of each of the men in this study, and understanding his own cultural context. These insights will enable us to make order out of this incredibly rich data.

Returning to the literature and looking ahead to the research

My review of the literature reveals a surprising uniformity in the research methods used by those who study men in the field of ECEC. By and large, the studies are attitudinal. Men in their pre-service training as well as those who work in the field, and sometimes their female colleagues, are asked to fill in questionnaires regarding their attitudes and experiences. Going one step further, many studies rely on interviews or focus groups to gather data on the important issues such as entry into the profession, difficulties and challenges in the work, and outcomes such as levels of job satisfaction. Of the 60 articles and books I have read in preparation for this study, I have found only one investigation that was based on classroom observations. This methodological limitation restricts our understandings to the verbal expressions of the survey respondents and interviewees. From these studies we can only deduce what the men actually do in the classroom from what they choose to tell about their practice. Self-reporting is often characterized as biased because it frames the data within the informant's wishes regarding what he wants the listener to hear or what he thinks the listener wants to hear.

A second critique of the literature on gender balance in ECEC relates to its cultural narrowness, a concern addressed at the beginning of the chapter. Each book and research study focuses on one country only, and no attention has been paid to cross-cultural comparisons of men who work with young children. Consequently we have not been afforded the richness of a cultural lens through which to examine the work of men in ECEC. The notion that men's caring styles differ from those of women needs to be examined with a cultural lens. If we want to claim universality regarding men's practice in ECEC, we need to observe how men behave with children in various societies. Only then may we get answers to the question of how culture affects men's practice in the early childhood classroom.

This study focuses on how men in different societies deal with the challenges of choosing a career of work with young children. I examine the lower age range of ECEC work, ages 0–6, in day care centres and kindergarten classes. In order to look closely at the work, attitudes, philosophy and practice of these men, I selected a research method that used observations and interviews to elicit maximum information about their practice and their thoughts. To broaden my perspective on their work, I gathered data not only from the men themselves, but also from their supervisors. To learn about the cultural influences on these men, I studied one teacher or caregiver in each of six countries. The next chapter describes the method I used.

Notes

[1] In Europe, the early childhood professionals refer to their work as Early Childhood Education and Care (ECEC), which encompasses both work in the nursery with infants and toddlers, teaching in preschools with 3–5-year-olds, and teaching children ages 6–8 in schools. In the United States, the profession is called Early Childhood Education (ECE). Academic departments that train these professionals and conduct research in the field use these same nomenclatures. In this book the acronym ECEC will be used exclusively.

[2] King refers to the US grades. For a correspondence of early childhood grades and ages in the other countries discussed in this book, see Appendix 4.

Chapter 2

Aims and research methods

When men cross the gender boundaries of their culture by choosing to work with young children, they not only challenge the conventions but also they open new possibilities for expanding the meaning and importance of this work (Nordberg, 2004; Oyler *et al.*, 2001). While the requirement for quality childcare and early education is universal, each society defines for itself the parameters of these important endeavours. By taking a close look at the professional lives of six men who have chosen to work with young children, I set out to discover why men select this trajectory for themselves, the hurdles they must jump to achieve their goals and their unique pedagogical contribution to the field. Each man's story is unique because his practice grows out of his own personality, life experience and cultural milieu. Nonetheless, comparison of their narratives and field descriptions proved fruitful. Young children in all societies require love and caring, they are curious about their world, and they seek to understand it through active engagement with the people in their surroundings and with the physical environment as well. Regardless of their culture, ECEC caregivers and teachers share the responsibility and privilege of responding to children's needs. This multiple case study addresses the important question of how men from different societies meet this responsibility and privilege, and looks at how they arrived at their decision to work in the field. The research seeks to reveal both the common and the particular meanings they find and create in their work.

The overarching aims of my research can be framed within personal, professional and socio-cultural contexts. I outline my goals as I formulated them at the outset of my research journey, and I delve into how these constructs developed and changed as I came to know these extraordinary men. Other critical factors that influenced my own growth as a researcher included reading, discussing gender-related issues with experts and scholars in the field and synthesizing these into a conceptual whole. I wanted to understand who the individual teachers are, what characterizes their personal trajectory of a career in ECEC and how they feel about their functioning in the early childhood classroom. I wanted to hear their stories as they chose to tell them. Through their narratives, I aimed to identify both internal and external influences. In addition, I was interested in their personal philosophy of early childhood education, how they view learning and how they think about care and caring for young children. As I listened to their narratives, I became interested in delving into theories of masculinity. On a deep level, I wanted to understand how these men construct their own masculinity and the extent to which their views of themselves as men play a central or more peripheral role in their professional self-identity. I was fascinated by the possibility that the personal constructs of masculinity relate both to their entry into the profession and their day-to-day work. I added an investigation of this question to my panoply of research goals.

Beyond my questions about these men as individuals, I was also interested in how they situated themselves in the classroom context with the children, parents and supervisors. I wanted to experience them at work with young children. I wished to learn about the quality of their relationships with the children and the special characteristics of the interactions that grow from their attention to the children's emotional and social needs. These connections included examples of the caring behaviour that the men exhibited, their empathy, use of touch, tone of speech and body language. I was curious as to how the men challenged the children cognitively in both formal and informal learning contexts, and how they addressed the children's emotional and social needs. I wanted to observe their communication with parents.

Another important aspect is their interactions with colleagues, including role divisions that define the work of day care and kindergarten teachers. Examining the learning environments they have created, learning how they equip the classroom and outdoor areas to achieve their own educational goals, and viewing the artefacts of their teaching and caregiving were important in my comprehension of the teacher in his work context. Beyond the design of the physical space of the learning environment, I wanted to know how they function in both static and dynamic surroundings. The dimension of time was also crucial to my research. I wanted to appreciate the flow of their day and how they pace activities and manage transitions throughout the day. To summarize, the classroom context centred on the men's relationship with the children as it found expression in the various domains of space and time.

Understanding the socio-cultural context in which these men function was perhaps the least tangible research goal but my most important one. I decided to create and use as many different lenses as possible to achieve insights at this level. I needed to listen carefully to the teacher's own narrative, which is steeped in his particular cultural context. Secondly, I viewed the institutions in which these men work to be an essential object of my investigation. I wanted to understand as much as possible about the culture of the school or centre, the norms of care, the expectations for school achievement, and the routines of teacher and caregiver interactions between themselves at an adult level. Thirdly, I wanted to reach out beyond the schools and the centres, to the broader culture as expressed by the neighbourhood, city, region or country. Learning about gender roles and gender equality in the different countries was as important to me as the localized cultures related to the school and day care centre. One of the forces driving this research was my passionate interest in how these broader social contexts influenced the first two circles of inquiry: the personal and the classroom.

Population

To achieve these multiple goals, I created a profile of the ideal subject for my study. The profile was rather lean: I wanted men who were both veteran ECEC teachers and interested in cooperating with the research plan at all stages. By limiting my research population to teachers with at least five years' work experience, I was able to focus on models of mature men who had chosen a career in ECEC and who viewed themselves as stable in their career. Many studies have pondered the revolving door nature of men's work in the ECEC classroom, citing the common phenomenon of men either leaving the profession (Jacobs, 1993) or moving up into administrative positions (Cameron, 2001). I wanted to understand why men choose to remain on the job, and I felt that identifying the characteristics of such men would contribute to scholarship in the field. In addition, I sought variety in the age levels at which the men were working, from toddlers to kindergarten. Although ECEC is usually defined as focusing on ages 0–8, I wanted to look at men who work with preschool children so I could fully explore the nature of caring and nurturing. One limitation of the study was language. I wanted to communicate easily with my subjects so I decided to forgo esoteric situations and select only men who spoke English as either a first or second language. The one exception was my Israeli subject, with whom I share the common language of Hebrew. With this profile as a guide, my next step was to narrow the list of countries that would serve as a basis for comparison.

My three goal contexts – the personal, the classroom and the society – determined the selection of countries to include in the study. Productive comparison of my subjects entailed choosing countries that are significantly different from one another both culturally and in terms of the participation of men in the early childhood workforce. On the other hand, I was limited by budget and travel possibilities, a reality that excluded distant continents such as Asia, Africa, South America and Oceana. Looking close to home, I chose to include my former country, the United States, and my current country, Israel, where I have lived for 25 years. Making the familiar strange is a respected, powerful tool in anthropological investigations of a local culture; and I have chosen to use it here by investigating these two countries from a new perspective. Attitudes towards gender roles differ greatly between Israel and America, with the former characterized by a more traditional stance.

Moving beyond my own playing field, I decided to take advantage of my travels in Europe, which had been related to academic activities such as conferences. Over the years I have come to appreciate the wide cultural differences between the European countries, so I chose four of these nations as venues for my research. Gender equality in the Scandinavian countries is far in advance of the other nations, Norway being well known as the most progressive in terms of social policy. Among all European nations, Norway has excelled in achieving the highest level of men participating in the ECEC workforce (Peeters, 2007). Switzerland stands out as a unique society considering the coexistence of very forward-thinking trends of sexual equality alongside very conservative practices such as women limiting their careers until their children have grown up (Federal Office for Gender Equality, 2008), which makes it an interesting case in its own right. In the UK, gender balance in education has received much public attention through policies and research (Peeters, 2007; Nutbrown, 2012), so I decided to add England. The Dutch situation differs somewhat in its open attitude towards sexual orientation (Stefans and Wagner, 2004) and gender equality on the one hand, and its conservative backdrop on the other (Achterberg and Houtman, 2009). So these six countries would be represented in the study: Israel, the USA, Norway, England, Switzerland and the Netherlands. As mentioned above, these choices excluded important and exciting parts of the world that were beyond my reach, and in which important steps have been taken to promote gender balance in teaching. With the countries selected, my next task was to find one willing subject from each.

Identifying subjects for my study was not as difficult as I had suspected when I was planning the research. My basic strategy was to contact professional and research colleagues in each country and to ask for their help in locating a man who had been teaching young children for a number of years. Everyone with whom I spoke was willing to help me with my project. While some had at least one teacher in mind as a candidate for the study, others referred me to professionals in the field whom they thought could help. In some cases I located the teacher directly; while in others I located a supportive day care director who found a member of the staff who agreed to participate in the study. Once I located the teacher, I asked permission from the immediate supervisor to conduct the observation. Restraining factors included geography, language and motivation. For example, in one case no teacher could be located in a city where I intended to travel; in another case

I was referred to a teacher in a small village who spoke little English; and in a third case several men who were approached by my colleague turned down the invitation to participate. After considerable legwork and correspondence across cyberspace, I succeeded in identifying six men who fitted my research profile, all of whom were pleased to be asked and were fervently cooperative.

A brief demographic description of the six selected teachers presents a surprisingly homogeneous group according to some factors and wide variation on others. Five of the men initiated their career with young children as student teachers or interns as part of their studies, and one began as a substitute teacher. The average age at which work with young children began was 24, with a range of 20 to 27. Because I sought a veteran profile, the average number of years of teaching was 12, with a range of 5 to 27. At the time of the interviews, the ages of my subjects stretched from 30 to 50, with an average of 37. As a group half were married or in a stable relationship, and half were bachelors. Two of the married teachers are fathers themselves.

Their work environments and job assignments can also be divided: four of the men teach 5–7-year-olds, referring to themselves as kindergarten teachers. The other two work in day care centres with toddlers aged 1–2, one calling himself a nursery caregiver and the other a pedagogic leader. While three kindergarten teachers (for ages 5–7) function in self-contained classrooms teaching alone or with an aide, one teacher in a private school teams with others at different times during the week. The two who teach in day care settings function strictly as team members; one is a pedagogic leader of the team while the other is of equal status to his colleagues. Both the kindergarten and toddler teachers have an on-site supervisor, the exception being the teacher at the private school, whose supervisor is the chairperson of a voluntary board of directors. The teachers have direct contact with the parents of the children with whom they work. This data is organized graphically in Appendix 1.

Data collection

I knew that I needed to spend uninterrupted time observing the teachers at work and to converse with them in a relaxed fashion for an extended period. Therefore, I decided to spend a day with each of my subjects in the school or day care centre, from the first child's arrival in the morning until the last child's departure at the end of the day. My observations lasted six to seven hours, although I used the teachers' breaks as an opportunity to speak with them and get answers to my many questions arising from my observation. This enabled me to observe the teacher's interactions with the children and with their parents at drop-off and pick-up times. I achieved my goal almost completely. I was granted permission by several to arrive before the children in order to meet and chat with the teachers as they engaged in their morning preparations. Others requested that I show up only after the morning was under way. In terms of pick-up, I found some children remained for an extended day programme, which precluded teacher–parent interaction. In the day care centres, the teachers' shifts ended before the children went home. In spite of these logistical limitations, I was able to observe some parent–teacher interaction at either the beginning or the end of the day.

In addition to the data about the teacher, I also wanted to learn about the socio-cultural context in which he worked. I needed to know the policies of the school on both hiring men and touch, and the attitudes of supervisors towards the desirability of having men on the staff. Therefore, I arranged a brief interview of a half hour to an hour with the immediate supervisor of each of the men in my study. When possible, these interviews took place during the school day while I was observing the teacher. I identified a time when the teacher was doing preparations or was less involved in direct interaction with the children to conduct these interviews. In two cases the supervisor was not present at the school on the day of my observation so I arranged for separate interviews with them, one by phone and one by meeting. The interviews focused on the supervisor's view of men working in ECEC, as well as their hiring practices. I was interested in their views about differences between men and women on the job, and how they understood men's contributions to the education of young children. I tapped their experience with parents' responses to finding a man in the early childhood classroom. These interviews also focused on the socio-cultural environment of the school in terms of the community in which the school was situated and the culture of the school or centre. Although each interview protocol was prepared to suit the situation, they followed a pattern. I have included one of these open-ended interview protocols in Appendix 3.

My method of data collection during the teachers' working hours was that of a non-participant observer. While free to move around the classroom and follow the teacher and children up close and far away, I typically found a spot to sit or stand in a corner of the room that afforded me a full sweep of the class and the ability to monitor the teacher's movements from one point to another. At times I moved in briefly to get a closer look at the interactions and the actual manipulation of materials and toys. This self-imposed arrangement prevented me from interfering with the teacher–child interaction – a methodological gold standard. While my eye was usually focused on the teacher himself, at times I turned my attention to the independent activities of the children, in order to absorb the culture of the classroom and understand how they functioned when the teacher was not interacting with them.

For four of the six subjects, I was granted permission to video record classroom activities. I filmed mainly the teacher interacting with the children, often using a zoom lens to capture the details of intimate or close interactions. I filmed for two to three hours of the six- to seven-hour day. I photographed all the classroom environments when children were not in the room, as a means of obtaining visual artefacts for further investigation. In the kindergarten classes, the teacher introduced me to the children as a visitor who wanted to learn about how they play. In the toddler rooms, no introduction was needed as the children paid me little attention. In the kindergarten classes too, the children typically ignored me. When they wished to show me something they were doing or had created, I agreed, nodding approval and trying to minimize my interactions with them. In addition, I wrote extensive field notes describing the teacher's interactions with the children and the flow of activities throughout the day. Where I did not speak the language of the classroom, I wrote notes about instances I wanted to understand better, and asked for interpretations at the end of the day or during the teacher's break. Within one day of my visit, I typed the field notes so I could organize my thoughts and further questions while the memories were still fresh.

Establishing a relationship of respect and trust with the teachers was a critical element of my research method (Schwalbe and Wolkomir, 2001). I accomplished this by several means. With the exception of the local Israeli teacher, I conducted a brief email correspondence with each, describing the research and its aims. I specified my requirements for inclusion in the study: a full day of observation and a three-hour interview at the end of the working day. I also asked for permission to video record the classroom events and made detailed arrangements for the visit. This correspondence was followed by a phone call about a month before my visit. I sought to establish a relaxed and trustful relationship with the teacher. One means of achieving trust was to assure him that he was in control of the data and its uses. In addition, he made all the critical decisions about my visit, permitting me to spend the day in his classroom, and deciding where I was allowed to be and when. I cannot recall any case of the teacher deliberately showing off by pointing out a particular aspect of the classroom or activity. Rather, they consistently left the selection of what to attend to in their classrooms to me.

For most of the visits, I shared a lunch break with the teacher, which gave us another opportunity to get acquainted and made a point of going beyond the research itself, with the aim of finding common interests. At the end of the day, the interviews were conducted in a relaxed manner, at a time and place suggested by the teacher. The venue was always quiet, away from the bustle of the school or centre activities, and uninterrupted by others. The interviews were digitally recorded and later transcribed for analysis.

These conversations began with an invitation for the teacher to tell his story in an unstructured narrative fashion, with minimal interruptions on my part. My planned protocol included a prompt that would trigger the narrative, followed by open-ended questions about topics that I predicted might not arise in the narrative (see Appendix 2). I began with the prompt: 'Could you tell me about how you came to the profession of nursery caregiver/ kindergarten teacher? What led you to this decision?' When the teacher had completed his story, I asked questions for clarification and probed for further breadth and depth on points that he had glossed over or not mentioned at all. A second major prompt invited an expansion on his narrative: 'When you think of your work as a nursery caregiver/kindergarten teacher, which experiences are most important to you?' I asked his views on the different contributions of men and women in ECEC and about gender differences in teaching. My last prompt looked to the future: 'Where do you see yourself ten years from now?' At the end, I referred to questions from my field notes written during my observation, asking for clarification of anything I wanted to understand better. While these prompts were brief, the resulting narratives were quite lengthy. In most cases I needed the entire three hours I had specified in advance for the interview. I ended the interviews by asking the subjects if they had any questions for me.

In order to broaden my perspective of the various cultures and the political climate and norms of gender balance in each country, I sought out scholars and practitioners in the field who either study gender balance or have involved themselves with relevant organizations on a regional or national level. Many had either initiated or were active in advocacy groups that promote gender balance in ECEC. I generally conducted interviews with these scholars and practitioners by telephone and they often referred me to relevant literature and data sources such as government reports.

Ethical considerations

Certain procedures were followed to ensure that the research met ethical standards. Each subject participated voluntarily in the study, and agreed to the full-day observation followed by a three-hour interview. All the teachers and their supervisors granted permission to use their full name and the name and location of their school or day care centre in the published results of the study. Likewise, I obtained permission from other interviewees to use their names, titles, and school or day care affiliation, and in four cases, the teachers' supervisors as well as the teachers themselves granted permission for me to video activities during my observation. In each case, a letter signed by me with the approval of the teacher and supervisor was sent to parents explaining the research project and asking for written permission to video the children for research purposes. In one centre two parents objected to the video recording so I turned on the camera only when their children were not present. At the beginning of each interview with the teachers, supervisors, scholars or gender balance practitioners in the field, I asked for permission to record the session. During the interviews themselves I accorded with the wishes of the interviewee and stopped the recording when they wished to say something off the record. Within two weeks of each interview, I sent the transcript to the interviewee, and asked for their approval of the document. In each case, the interviewee made revisions to the transcript about their intentions and factual corrections.

Once I had completed each chapter, I sent a draft to the teacher requesting revisions or corrections. This usually entailed two or three revisions before the subject granted his permission in writing to publish the chapter. I waited until the teacher had approved the chapter before showing it to his supervisor so the teacher maintained control over material written about him. After making the requested revisions, I obtained written permission from these informants also. All children's names used in the chapters are pseudonyms chosen to reflect the culture of the children's families. I obtained permission from the school or centre authority to use these pseudonyms, after being assured that no child with those particular names had ever attended the school or centre. These procedures assured privacy for the children being observed, and afforded the teachers and other informants full control over the publication of the part of the manuscript related to themselves and their institution.

Data analysis

In his book entitled *Gender*, Connell (2002) raises the difficulties and challenges of ethnography as a research method, particularly with respect to the mass analysis of observational data. Connell states: 'You need to know what you are looking for. But you also need to be open to new experiences and new information, able to see things that you did not expect to see' (ibid.: 13). Throughout the observations, interviews and analysis, I tried to open myself to the unexpected – and I was richly rewarded. I altered my original research questions to include topics that arose from the observations, both in learning about ECEC in various cultures and learning how the men function in their settings. In particular, I continued to be amazed at similarities between the men's viewpoints, even in the way they expressed their ideas.

The data analysis method used in preparing the chapters on each teacher, and that used in preparing the final chapter comparing the six subjects, are described separately. For the individual chapters on the teachers, I reread my field notes of the observation, watched the video recordings, and reviewed the still pictures of the classroom environments. In addition, I used those portions of the interview transcript in which I asked the teacher to interpret for me certain events of the morning that I had not quite understood. This procedure followed the ethnographic research paradigm of writing a thick description (Schon, 1983) of a day in the teacher's classroom. I was able to distil the essential characteristics and style of each teacher, and bring evidence from the observation to support these claims. Triangulation was obtained by cross-referencing the observed events against the different data sets mentioned above. While the men's style of teaching on a cognitive level was of central importance, I also looked closely at their modes of communication and caring and their responsiveness to the children's emotional and social needs. Thus I was able to capture those elements of their work with the children as an essential part of the role of caregiver and teacher of young children.

My research questions framed the analysis of the various data sets I collected. The initial research goal focused on learning about internal and external influences on these men's career decision, and its continuation by their remaining in the profession. Thus, in preparing the teacher's own narrative for his individual chapter, I coded the interviews based on elements of his career trajectory, including the initial decision-making, training and job history. I created a timeline for each teacher, so that I could fit those pieces into an accurate sequence. Another important aspect of the teacher's story was the reactions of family and friends to his decision to work with young children. Elements of the transcript that shed light on this issue were also coded. After I wrote the trajectory piece of the narrative, I added questions for the teacher related to lacunae in the narrative, or details such as locations and institutions. I submitted the draft of each chapter to the teacher for comments, including requests for any further information needed to complete the picture. I used methods of narrative analysis as described by Andrews *et al.* (2008) looking for recurring themes, key words, repetitions and omissions. This narrative analysis enabled me to describe how the teacher himself thought about his story, and what meaning it had for him, both in the past and in the present. My search for themes in the trajectory material constituted a first level of analysis based on how the teachers presented their story, along with further information that I was able to draw out based on additional questions.

A second, and more analytical, piece of the research relates to my research goals about the men's feelings and perceptions of themselves as early childhood educators and particularly as men doing this job. These research questions deal specifically with their personal philosophy of early childhood education and their professional identity as an early childhood educator. To address these research goals, I looked closely at the reflective material included in the semi-structured interviews, which followed their initial narrative about their career. These reflections represent a metacognitive level of the men's understanding of their own narrative. In addition, I wanted to write about their views of their own masculinity, both personal and professional. I sought to understand how they saw gender differences both in their own workplace and in the early childhood profession in general. This analysis of their masculinity also called for a higher level of abstraction by me as a researcher, over and above my analysis of their personal narrative and my description of a day in their classroom. Thus I recoded the interview transcript based on the categories mentioned above: philosophy of early childhood education, professional identity, masculinity and attitudes about gender differences in the classroom. I corroborated my conclusions on these issues as far as possible with behaviour that I had observed in the classroom from memory, field notes and video recordings.

The comparative analysis in the final chapter was based on further coding and categorizing the data sets from each teacher. At this level, I reread the chapters and drew from them recurrent themes that would enable me to compare and contrast the six teachers. I created a matrix with the categories on the vertical and the teachers' names on the horizontal axis. I began with a limited number of *a priori* categories such as reason for choosing the profession, personal philosophy of ECEC, touch and masculinity. I found these classifications inadequate for comparing and contrasting the six subjects. Using grounded theory (Strauss and Corbin, 2008), I generated new categories as I reread the chapters, ending up with 35 labels, which I later collapsed and synthesized to ten. In writing the final chapter, I took into consideration the findings according to these more encompassing nodes of analysis, enabling me to draw broad conclusions about my subjects. This synthesis included both similarities and differences between the teachers according to major themes such as influences on entering and leaving the profession, the ethos of caring, personal and professional self-identity, work with parents, work with children, thoughts about gender and working with young children, construction of masculinity and issues about touching children. Whenever possible, for each of these comparisons, I enlisted theory to understand the similarities and differences between the teachers and to suggest cultural explanations where they seemed relevant.

Having introduced the theoretical basis of studying men in ECEC and my methods of investigation, I now enter the professional worlds of my six subjects, and learn about their past and their hopes for the future.

Chapter 3

Benny Haidlauf

Kindergarten Teacher, Israelitische Gemeinde Kindergarten
Basel, Switzerland

'This profession helps me keep my little child in me.'

Benny's user name on his email address is 'magicben', a name that captures
his sense of wonder, his enthusiastic satisfaction with his work and his
extraordinary connection with the children he teaches. His decision to become
a kindergarten teacher was quite deliberate. He knew throughout high school
that he would not follow his parents' advice to become a clarinettist. However,
it took him many years from completing his compulsory army service at
age 19 before he signed up for a kindergarten teacher training course at 27.
In between he worked as a clerk in a music store, then as a salesman, and
for several years as a customer service agent for an international transport
service. Although this last job comfortably supported his bachelor lifestyle,
he felt unfulfilled in the work. As he told me, he came home one day and
asked himself: 'What did you do today?' and his answer fell far short of
his vision for his current life and for his future. Shortly afterwards he saw
a newspaper advert for a kindergarten teacher training programme, and he
decided to apply. He reflected on his job at the transport company, comparing
it to the role of the kindergarten teacher: 'The smile on the face of a child – it
was better than three months of work [at the transport company].'

His decision was driven by an extended background of work with
children in the Catholic church where his father served as a deacon. The
church was located in the small town of Arlesheim, where he grew up. As
a teen, he had led youth activities in the church, an experience that set the
tone for his resolution to become a preschool teacher. Once accepted to the
education programme, he quit his well-paid job, took out loans, and began
two years of study as one of two men in a class of 30 at the Kantonalen
Lehrerseminar in Basel-Stadt.

The practical aspects of the training programme were valuable to him,
as he learned didactic skills, engaged in student teaching, wrote reflectively,
and learned how to manage a preschool class. The more theoretical courses
were less appealing to him. Although Benny draws a clear distinction between
adults and children, he cherishes what he calls 'the child in me' as central to his
identity as an early childhood educator. He described his training programme

in this way: 'So [the course] was mainly methodic [teaching methods] … how to make and introduce themes, how you can approach the kids. We are all adults, with my child in me I am an adult. You have to change your thinking, so that was helpful. So the best way is learning by doing, [as well as] the reflection, that's important.'

Upon completing his training, he worked as the first male kindergarten teacher in a small town, before moving to Basel, where he was the first male teacher in the public preschool system. He worked as a substitute teacher for five years before receiving his own kindergarten class, where he remained for two years. As a teacher in the public sector, he was placed in a school serving immigrant populations largely from Turkey. Eleven years into his career, he married another kindergarten teacher whom he met at a professional gathering. As the number of students decreased and schools were shut down, his hours were cut by 50 per cent. Unable to support his family on this reduced salary, he decided to look elsewhere for a job. His wish was answered when he saw a newspaper advert for a teacher in the Jewish community kindergarten in Basel. He was hired despite his Catholic background because of his competence as an early childhood educator and because of his expertise in teaching the state curriculum, which is used in the parochial school as well. He commented about the job change: 'This is something new and a chance to learn another world, there is a pull and a push.'

Philosophy of teaching

Because he was not totally confident that he could express his ideas clearly in English, Benny asked if he could bring his colleague, Lea Karger, to translate for him. During our two-hour conversation one day and an additional hour the next, we delved into a number of topics. But when I read the transcript, I realized that Benny spoke more eloquently and passionately about his personal philosophy of working with young children than about anything else. It was apparent that he had clearly formulated ideas about educating young children, and he was eager to express them. First of all he stressed the importance of understanding the world from the child's point of view. 'In [my] profession I see through the eyes of the children. I see new things, this and that, which normal adults don't see … I take it as normal.' He treats children with respect, and aims to make them feel that they are important. Listening attentively is a major component of showing respect. He explained his genuine interest in the children's ideas: 'In the morning, a child told me something. I could say to myself "Ah, so boring." But instead, I ask the child again and again, to show her [how interested I am in her ideas]. There's nothing that's not important.'

His theory of learning combines both modelling and co-construction of knowledge. He achieves his role as a provider of information by sitting with the children so they can learn by his showing them things, helping them and making direct eye contact. He expanded on this approach:

> We are very important persons for this time in the child's life. What I think, what I say, what I do, what I live, so that's all important. You can give them images of life. You can give them pictures of how to act, how to interact, yes.

But teaching for him is not only providing a role model and transferring knowledge from his brain to theirs, rather it is a matter of mediation in which he helps the children find and release their own creativity. He explained how he scaffolds the development of children's fantasy worlds by engaging himself with their play: 'When they play with Lego, they bring 2–3 blocks [and then] they are finished. So you sit with the children two, three days and hear their stories and [bring out their] fantasy-like ideas.' He offered a further example of mediation in the realm of creative arts: 'Also the paper cuts, I show them one thing which they can do … and they go on with their (own) construction, and all of a sudden it comes from them.'

Music is important to Benny. 'I love to sing, I love to play guitar. As a musician I encourage fantasy and creativity.' This fondness for music became immediately apparent to me when I first entered his classroom and noticed his guitar displayed on a stand in the meeting area. I was rewarded for my observation during the morning meeting, which Benny concluded with a round of singing and dancing. He enthusiastically led the group, singing with guitar accompaniment, as he integrated movement and dance, to the delight of all the children. I needed no translator to understand what they were singing about. He also brought out his guitar at the end of the day. After the children had put on their street shoes and were sitting in the foyer waiting to go home, he did a round of songs that brought the group together, provided a physical outlet through creative movement, and provided him total control.

Our discussion about his philosophy of education revealed Benny's intense interest in the child's world and his passion for working closely with the children, individually and collectively, to enable them to realize their creative potential. For him the ideal relationship with the child is an integration of authority and equality. Benny's child orientation drives his thinking about the role of adults in the education of young children. Far from laissez-faire, he espouses active engagement based on his own agenda as well as the child's. Although he may initiate a focus for the child's inquiries, he will just as readily accept the child's choice of content or line of reasoning. Building on this basic interest and motivation of the child, Benny adds his own enthusiasm, questions and creativity to blend with the child's. His bottom line is respect, a word he uses frequently when describing his relationship with the children. He eloquently summed up his attitude towards work with the children: 'I want to show them that I can be the boss, but I'm also their friend. It's like a partnership.'

Two mornings in Benny's class

My observation took place in the Jewish kindergarten on the grounds of the Jewish community building and synagogue in Basel. The school has experienced a reduction in students over the years as the community has dwindled. Benny is in charge of the kindergarten class of six children, and works with Lea, a Judaic specialist who teaches about holidays, prayers and Bible stories. In addition, he team-teaches with another non-Jewish teacher who is in charge of the 3- and 4-year-olds. The two groups regularly come together at certain points each day although most of the daily activities are organized separately in two very large, well-appointed, early childhood classrooms. At the time of our interview Benny had been working in this private kindergarten for seven months.

This theme of being childlike, of entering into the children's play, and nurturing the 'little child within' is central to Benny's professional self-identity. Although he doesn't favour imposing himself on the children, he is totally available to them during their play. I observed him during a free play session on two consecutive days, and found him to be completely engaged with the children in a playful yet respectful manner, encouraging their autonomy while supporting their immediate needs. There follows several examples of his warm and encouraging approach to the children.

The outdoor recess lasted for an hour, during which time he never stopped for a break. The playground is minimally equipped with a large climbing structure. There is a storage chest with modular elements for gross motor play including sections of logs, planks and ropes, which Benny brought to the school. When the children first arrived at the playground, he took the equipment out of the chest for the children to use. As they began constructing obstacle paths, ramps and rope connections according to their own plans, Benny offered other suggestions to provide more physically challenging constructions. The interaction was involving yet relaxed. It was difficult to distinguish between the children's and Benny's initiatives, as both were clearly enjoying the ensuing play.

Despite the small number of children in the group, someone was always left out. Benny took special care to approach these 'loners'. Sometimes he played with the child and at other moments he found ways of helping them connect with peers through physical activity. In contrast to the teacher of the 3- and 4-year-olds, who took a more passive and observational role, Benny was proactive throughout the entire hour of recess. Later on in our conversation, Benny explained to me that he had initiated equipping the playground with these modular items to give the children stimulating gross motor activities. These playground scenes illustrate Benny's leadership role in enhancing the learning environment, and his active involvement with the children in their play.

Upon entering the classroom after recess, the children sat down at a large table for a spring art project, creating flowers for a collage. Benny encouraged each child to design her own flowers using petals pre-cut from coloured paper. Sometimes he helped them by squeezing out glue from a stiff bottle, while the child designated where the glue needed to go on the paper. The creative work was clearly the child's, with Benny acting as facilitator for bringing their ideas to fruition. My attention was drawn to two children who had cut spectacles out of paper, decorated them, and were trying to fit them onto their faces. Benny joined their game, examining the spectacles and trying them on in humorous positions on his own face. At the request of one of the children, he cut a hole in the paper so the child could execute her plans. As other children finished their flowers, he consulted them about where on the window to place them as classroom decorations. This activity illustrates how Benny scaffolds the learning experience, providing a clear structure while encouraging individual creativity and responsiveness.

A third example of his involvement with the children was evident in the show and tell session that Benny organizes every Friday as a special event following the morning's pre-Sabbath ritual of prayer and a fancy meal. This is designed to prepare the children for the actual Sabbath events they will experience at home and in the synagogue that evening or the next day. During my visit, the religious events were led by his Jewish colleague, while he took a more functional role in preparing and serving the food, and helping the children dress up as adult family members for the Sabbath festivities. The events took place with the two groups combined. Afterwards he and Lea organized the 5-year-olds in a circle for the weekly show and tell activity. This important event was conspicuously Benny's turf, as he took the leadership role, while Lea was more passively involved. As each child revealed their treasure from home, Benny asked questions that supported the child's thinking about their object. Benny showed intense interest in each artefact and about the stories that the children told about their special offering. After each child had shown, talked about and demonstrated their object, Benny encouraged the children to share their objects in play with their classmates. Benny too played with the toys under the guidance of the children who brought them. He clearly enjoyed each interaction, and his playfulness reflected his overall delight at the opportunity to explore a unique aspect of each child's world that they had chosen to share with their friends. Benny related to each object as though it were totally new to him.

Emotion and nurturance

Benny's conception of caring is well formulated. He understands that it is his responsibility to support the emotional needs of the children while always encouraging them to move forward with their own agendas. I observed that his support was expressed physically, with a pat, a touch, or a show of concern. More important was his verbal response, his empathetic looking the child in the eye while inviting their story, 'What happened?' His body language demonstrated another dimension of his caring attitude towards the children. He spent a great deal of time squatting or bending down to the children's level, rarely speaking to them from his full height.

When I asked Benny about differences between men and women in their approach to children, he replied that the children seek out a female teacher when they are in emotional distress and want to be comforted physically. When children fall and hurt themselves, they approach Benny for comfort if no woman is present. In such cases, he listens and prompts them to try again, sending them back to challenge themselves in the same task, but this time with his backing and encouragement. Benny believes that his approach encourages their positive emotional, social and physical development. His support, with its way of gently pushing the children forward, characterizes men's unique contributions to the early childhood classroom.

During my day and a half of observation, I witnessed several incidences of Benny's supportive response to children's emotional displays. During the show and tell activity, Rebecca revealed a heavy metal medallion to her friends in the group. As she placed it around her neck, the pendant struck her face causing some pain. Her tears were met with Benny's comforting voice, a gentle stroke to her cheek, and practical suggestions for wearing it safely. As her tears dried up, Rebecca explained the medallion's significance to the group.

At the end of the day as the children were engaged in the closing activity, Aliza began to cry as she stood among the group at the bottom of the stairs where her mother would pick her up. Benny approached her, put his hands on her cheeks, and spoke softly, asking what had happened. He then continued with his announcements for the end of the day, dealing with last-minute issues such as forgotten items, shoe tying and reminders about what to bring the following week. Noticing that Aliza was still tearful, he approached her a second and third time, again offering a pat on the cheek, squatting down to her level to offer comfort. His repeated measures paid off. Aliza's tears turned to smiles and she departed in a cheerful mood. In both incidents, Benny offered empathy in a controlled fashion. His response was heavily verbal, using physical touch only slightly. He communicated to Rebecca and Aliza that he recognized their pain, yet he also conveyed a clear message that they needed to move forward and get back on track.

Benny demonstrated caring through small gestures as well as through his keen interest and involvement in the children's play. During the free play time, he moved from child to child, finding for each one the optimal play venue for that moment. When he began working at the synagogue kindergarten, he acquired a large quantity of Lego, which he arrayed on a wide table on one side of the main room. This well-equipped venue invited children to build, play and display their work over time. Benny is intrigued with this type of construction, and will often play with a child at the Lego table for long periods, building together, discussing the construction and playing with their creations.

His involvement with the children's art work is yet another vehicle for his deep interest in the children themselves. While observing Benny's delight in playing with the children, I got the impression that if he had been 30 years younger, he would have been extremely pleased to engage himself in the rich, stimulating learning environment he had set up for the children. The manner in which he served food at the snack table marked an additional sign of caring. He went around the table, personally offering each child a cracker and a selection of fruit that he arranged attractively on a tray. After the first round, he made a second offering with equal care and attention. For Benny, each child is important and each deserves his special attention, which he makes certain to provide.

Masculinity and professional identity

'I'm not a woman,' Benny stated emphatically when I asked him how the role of a man might differ from that of a woman in the kindergarten. His near hostile response to my question almost derailed my reasoning for trying to understand his views on gender roles in the preschool class. But after probing further, I succeeded in understanding his views on the matter and could appreciate how he constructs his masculinity in his professional role as a kindergarten teacher. Foremost is his conviction that clear gender modelling benefits both boys and girls. For him, the ideal situation is having a man work beside a woman, each modelling their own gender-appropriate role. 'They have mom and dad – they have a female and a male. That is the best for the child.'

Benny's prior experience in the Basel public kindergarten informed his understanding of the benefits of men teaching young children. Most of his pupils there were Turkish immigrants, many of whom lived with only their mother. For those children, he was 'the part that was missing'. The single mothers appreciated their children having a man teacher, and the fathers who were present were able to communicate with him in ways that would not have been possible with a woman. Benny told me the surprising statistic that 27 men were working as kindergarten teachers in the Basel schools when he was employed there. Jonathan Amato, a coordinator of early childhood education from Basel Public Schools, confirmed that in 2012 out of a total of 270 kindergarten teachers, 24 were men. 'When we hire men, the only question we ask them is how they are going to manage with the fact that they are doing "a woman's job".' He added that it would be ideal if they could achieve total gender balance with a 50 per cent male workforce.

On the two days of my visit Benny presented himself in the classic masculine garb of jeans, T-shirt and trainers. His outward manly appearance was reflected in his vivid descriptions of alpine vacations where snowboarding was the major focus. He fondly described ski weekends in his bachelor days that he arranged with the other men kindergarten teachers in Basel, in which skiing and male camaraderie provided mutual support.

At the beginning of this part of our conversation he was unwilling to consider how he might bring unique male traits to the kindergarten other than providing the presence of a man for both deprived and privileged children. As the interview continued, he acknowledged differences in terms of how the teacher relates to children, particularly in situations of stress. He said revealingly: 'Normally women are weaker and softer, and men perhaps more [silent pause]. If a child falls down or something, a woman will accept [the crying, but] a man will say "It's okay, it will happen again, but it's going to be good."' At this point in the interview, Benny and Lea (colleague and translator) spoke between themselves in German, working out what happens when a stressed child cries. They ended up agreeing on the following description of their own modus operandi as well as the children's behaviour. To my delight, Benny summarized their discussion for me in English:

I think the child thinks that a woman will more readily come to his assistance when under stress [Benny demonstrates with a crying outburst]. But I come also, even though the children don't expect it. But when I'm alone, the children decide for themselves. If it's really really important, then they cry and come to me. But if Lea is here, they don't consider whether it is important or not, they just cry because they know that she will take care of it.

Benny describes his approach as more business-like and effective in that he works very hard to 'bring the story to the ground' to find out what really happened. He believes that these differences in responding to emotionally stressful situations are indicative of differences between men and women in the kindergarten. The woman immediately responds on an emotional level, while the man takes the child seriously, showing respect, and reacts as appropriate. The man will pull the child up from his crisis and encourage her to move forward, try again, and return to the challenging situation instead of avoiding it. He will use this crisis as a learning situation to promote the child's resilience. When he described his views on the psychology courses he was required to take in his training programme, Benny emphasized his disdain for delving into emotions: 'Sure there are many unnecessary things [courses], so we have to sit there and listen, and [they] are not really interesting. Psychology: feel me touch me, *bah* [laughs]. So that's not my thing.'

Community and society

The Jewish community kindergarten in Basel is run by a volunteer board of directors. At the time of my visit, Dr Eric Odenheimer served as president. When his children were younger they attended the school, thus Eric's communal service is based on his personal commitment to the school as well as his desire to serve the needs of young families in the Jewish community. I was curious about the decision to hire a man for the position of kindergarten teacher, so I interviewed Eric to learn about the communal context of Benny's work. He shared with me his thinking at the time of Benny's job application: 'I had actually two thoughts. The one was curiosity: What type of man is this to be a kindergarten teacher? [My second thought was:] Do we have increased risks for sexual harassment when hiring a male teacher?' Upon further investigation including contact with Benny's former supervisor, Eric was satisfied on both counts. He concluded: 'I didn't find anything which would make me believe that we would have a problem here.' His overall assessment of Benny's work in the kindergarten was positive. He told me 'I like him as a personality.' He indicated that Benny challenges the children in positive ways that differ from those used by women, and that the children like him. Eric's sentiments were echoed in feedback that he received from parents, who stated that it was 'courageous to employ a man and that [having a male teacher] is good for the children.' He was surprised to hear such an enthusiastic response 'because actually I would have thought from the parent's side there would be more reluctance'. In order not to discriminate by gender, Eric felt it would be inappropriate to suggest guidelines for Benny regarding his touching the children, lap sitting and the like. He added that Benny is never alone with the children, and this forestalls concerns about issues of sexual abuse by all members of the staff. When I asked about differences between Benny and the female staff, Eric noted that Benny exercises extreme caution in matters of touching, hugging and lap sitting, perhaps as a self-imposed measure to prevent accusations.

Benny confirmed Eric's observations about his taking precautions. In our interview I asked him about what he does when a child needs help in the toilet, and he responded:

> If I have to do it, I do it, if I don't have to do it, meaning somebody else is here or in the other room … I'd rather ask them. Just to be secure. It's not really a concern … but it can affect me. First comes the child then comes the rest [laughs].

During my visit to the kindergarten, I did not observe Benny showing signs of overt physical affection to the children. On the other hand, he demonstrated deep interest in their thoughts, ideas and emotions, which he expressed by stooping to their level, engaging them in conversation and touching them lightly on the head or shoulder.

Benny perceived his initial reception by the parents differently to Eric. It was Benny who reported that because of widespread media coverage of paedophilia cases, parents were at first afraid of having a man in the kindergarten. But he did not let their fears bother him. He explained to me how he dealt with these issues: 'I leave the door open, and give them my phone number. I let them see how I work with the children.' By the time I visited the kindergarten, the parental fears had changed to admiration and respect.

To broaden my perspective of the social context in which Benny functions, I spoke to three activists and a researcher, all of whom deal with issues of gender balance. Lu Decurtins has spent the past 20 years trying to improve the lives of boys by increasing the presence of men in their lives, founding at least three organizations to this end. His first endeavour involved working with fathers to encourage them to take a more active role in their boys' upbringing. The second organization he co-founded, the Netzwerk

Schulische Bubenarbeit (NWSB, Network for Boys' Work in Schools), serves the needs of boys in school through several channels including professional development workshops for school personnel aimed at enhancing their understanding of the needs of boys. This network also strives to attract more men into the field of early childhood education, which Lu sees as a critical need. Two of Lu's colleagues, Urs Urech and Ron Halbright, are affiliated with the NWSB. Urs works in the field as a teacher trainer in gender awareness and Ron co-founded NWSB, serves on the board and produces educational materials. Each spoke to me separately about issues of men in Swiss ECEC settings, shedding light on the context of Benny's career. Wiebke Tennhoff is a PhD candidate at St Gallen University, and part of a research team investigating gender aspects in nurseries and 'whether male preschool teachers bring alternative forms of interaction to the nursery' (Nentwich and Vogt, 2012).

The situation for men who want to work with young children in Switzerland is both good and bad. On the positive side, urban parents are generally 'tickled' to have their young children cared for or taught by a man. Urs added: 'Parents are happy, they feel special that the kindergarten teacher is a male.' This attitude comes to the fore particularly among single mothers, who appreciate having a male role model 'who will play football with the boys and do other male things'. Getting trained and obtaining a diploma has been made easier in the last years by the establishment of an equal opportunities contact person in each Pädagogische Hochschule around the country. Managers of the day care nurseries (Kinderkrippen) as well as school principals are eager to hire men, which may indicate that institutional roadblocks to male employment in the field have been largely removed. Wiebke reported that of the 20 nursery managers whom her research team interviewed, only one stated that she would not hire a man to work in the nursery, in contrast to the generally positive attitude of the others.

This seemingly encouraging trend towards hiring men is tempered by limitations that are sometimes placed on male caregivers, particularly regarding the changing of nappies. This favourable environment for hiring men corroborates the relative ease with which Benny found employment nine years previously in the Basel schools and one year earlier in the Jewish kindergarten. With such encouraging social conditions, I began to wonder why the numbers of men in Swiss ECEC settings are so low, at 1 per cent in the kindergartens and only slightly higher in the preschools. When I turned to a Swiss colleague who taught at the Pädagogische Hochschule in Lucerne to help with my research by identifying a man who works with young children, she could only think of one whom she had encountered during the many years of her college teaching. They are extremely rare.

Lu indicated that over the years there has been a decrease in the number of men working in primary education as well as in the kindergartens. This was confirmed by data from the Swiss Federal Statistical Office (SFSO), which indicated that the percentage of men in the primary schools dropped from 29.3 in 1998/99 to 18.5 in 2012. In the kindergartens the percentage during the same years increased from 0.6 to 3.4 (SFSO, 2004; SFSO, 2012a). Lu gave two reasons for this downward trend: salary and status. Although pay for preschool work has remained stable over the years, it has not kept pace with salaries in other areas of employment. In addition, the formerly high status of teachers employed in village schools in the past has eroded, as teachers find themselves working in the cities under less favourable conditions. Lu elaborated on this point: 'Teaching is anonymous, hard work. You have to cooperate; you are no longer king of your class; you must cooperate with other professionals; you can't make your own decisions.' Eric Odenheimer also spoke about the relatively low status of kindergarten teachers. He explained that in Switzerland the participation of women in a profession correlates with lower status, using the example of physicians, whose status has dropped in line with the massive entry of women into the medical profession.

Ron suggested that the decrease in the number of men teaching in the schools is likely to continue. As the men currently working retire, they will not be replaced by other men. Ron added that until a series of changes around ten years ago, which included the academicization of the teaching profession, kindergarten and elementary teachers were masters in their own class, and the function of school principal did not exist. 'In the villages the school teacher was right below mayor in terms of status. Now teachers are public servants like everyone else.' The academicization limits the eligible pool of teacher candidates to the top 20 per cent of high school graduates. These same high achievers have career options that are more attractive. Women still choose teaching because it is family-friendly. It provides part-time, relatively well-paid work with school vacations, and the possibility of taking a break for several years without fear of job termination. Ron further explained that men tend not to value these career features in teaching, preferring more lucrative options.

Most of the male caregivers in Wiebke's study reported rather positive parental reactions towards them, along with some moments of mistrust. For example, they would 'first go to the female teacher instead of the male, while taking a look at how the man is doing the job'. Four out of nine caregivers were forbidden at some point to change nappies. Lu offered a psychological perspective: 'It's always like this when something is unknown. You are afraid of it.' One aspect of the mistrust of men relates to the disproportionate attention paid by the media to child abuse cases. During my visit to Switzerland my local hostess in Zurich pointed out a front-page article in the newspaper related to a child abuse case that had just come to light. The article sparked public debate about the appropriateness of allowing men to work with young children. Urs thought that concerns about child abuse are more prevalent in the nurseries with very young children than in kindergarten, which begins at age 5. As he mentioned in his narrative, Benny himself takes extreme caution with issues of touching children and avoids isolating himself with a child. Lu suggests that such an extreme position distorts the generally enlightened attitude of the Swiss towards men in ECEC; however, he admits that contrary views still persist.

Another consideration that weighs in as a difficulty for men in ECEC is the friction between women and men working together in the preschool classroom. This issue was illustrated in a story Lu told me about an in-service workshop he conducted for a group of women kindergarten teachers. He asked them what it would be like to work with a man in their classroom. They responded unanimously with laughter. They told him that the man would create chaos among the children, that the room would be dirty, and that the children would fight with each other. Some of them had worked with an inexperienced young man, who indeed had precipitated disorder. His questionable reputation had spread among the women, who were convinced that all men teachers lack the ability to conduct an orderly and clean classroom. Lu further analysed the almost inevitable abrasion between women and men in the Swiss ECEC classroom. He suggested that women who choose this work tend to be conservative in nature. In contrast, the men who select the profession are special; they are iconoclasts who have already broken out of the gender mould. Lu sees this combination as inherently problematic in his gender-oriented in-service teacher training programmes.

The Swiss government has supported a small project with the goal of increasing the number of men teaching young children (kindergarten to third grade). From 2005 to 2011, the Federal Office of Gender Equality supported the project 'Men into the lower grades!' (Männer in die Unterstufe!) within the framework of the Network for Boys' Work in Schools. This programme has developed a rich array of activities, flyers, short films and an attractive website. They have developed a mentoring programme whereby interested candidates can spend a day in another man's classroom. An additional facet of their programme involves an interface with the teachers' colleges,

Pädagogische Hochschulen, to encourage the staff to promote men teaching younger children. They are also active in the public debate about men in teaching. However, the effort to attract men into working with the younger children is at odds with rooted social forces. Now that the status of teachers has dropped sharply over the years, the prestigious academic high schools do not encourage their students to choose teaching in the kindergarten or primary school as a career, and are not eager to open their doors to activists from NWSB like Urs, who would like to show their wares at school job fairs and speak to young men about the possibility of choosing a career teaching young children.

Gender roles in Switzerland

The conservative nature of Swiss society explains a great deal of the cultural context in which Benny operates. Gender equality has been a long time coming in Switzerland. Women were only given the right to vote in 1971, making Switzerland the last industrial democracy to achieve universal suffrage. In the past men (and the society as a whole) expected their wives to stay at home and care for their preschool children, and continue to be at home during the elementary years to provide a hot lunch in the middle of the day. However, in the past ten years this attitude has changed for middle-class urban families, as women have entered the workforce, mostly in part-time jobs. Ron explained that children whose mothers work longer hours are cared for in a supplementary programme, called a 'Hort', which provides care before and after school hours, as well as a hot lunch. However, mothers who choose this option five days a week are often judged harshly by their communities. He surmised: 'Switzerland changes slowly. It's a consensual system. People can block change. Things don't get done and undone; they get done and stay done. It's taken here as a sign of quality that women are at home with their children. It's considered by most people to be good for the development of the child and good for Swiss society.' Other voices have countered such traditional attitudes, arguing that young women wish to keep involved in their work, earn their own money, and pursue their own careers.

The mother's dominant role in childcare in Swiss society can be understood by considering several social factors. The enforcement of traditional gender norms is strengthened by a historical background of universal discrimination against girls in school until the 1980s, particularly pronounced in Catholic and rural regions of the country (Praz, 2006). Furthermore, sex segregation in the workforce is a barrier to women's mobility in Swiss society (Hong Li *et al.*, 1998). Young women tend to be streamed into traditional women's professions, particularly in the nonacademic vocational tracks (Gonon *et al.*, 2001). The young Swiss mother confronts additional realities that encourage her to drop out of the workforce or work part-time. Significant numbers of Swiss women in their thirties withdraw from employment for several years to raise their children (Federal Office for Gender Equality, 2008).

In 2012, 78 per cent of working women were employed part-time and 29 per cent full-time (SFSO, 2013). There are very few Kinderkrippen (day care centres) and subsidized slots, and the full tuition for an infant at a Kinderkrippe amounts to 50.1 per cent of the average family net income (Rogers, 2012). According to the OECD (2012), only 22 per cent of children aged 3 attend these centres. 'There is still the belief that children should stay at home with their mothers.'

A society that fails to provide adequate childcare for young children is clearly ambivalent about women participating fully in the workforce. The Swiss national policy for childbirth parental leave was only recently adopted and is one of the least favourable among high-income nations. In its report on the topic, the Center for Economic and Policy Research in Washington provides a gender equality index, based on paid and unpaid leave for both parents and the incentives offered to take the leave. Swiss mothers are offered 14 weeks of paid leave and may request longer unpaid, but there are no benefits for fathers; whereas Sweden offers mothers 47 weeks' paid leave and another 116 unpaid, and fathers 7 paid weeks and 71 unpaid (Ray *et al.*, 2008). This data indicates Switzerland's lack of support for paternal involvement in childcare and discouragement of women with children from actively participating in the workforce. That women stay out of the workforce during their childbearing years fits with rigid gender stereotyping regarding occupational choice. Social pressures on women begin with gender discrimination in school, continue by steering women's occupational choices to traditional female roles, and are confirmed by the restrictive policy on leave at childbirth and the dearth of adequate and affordable day care for young children.

Although the cultural norm in Switzerland is for mothers to take an active part in the care of their young children, in 2011, 41 per cent of children aged 4 and 94 per cent of children aged 5 attended kindergarten (SFSO, 2012b: 2). As participation in the kindergarten has increased, the programme has also shifted. Ron explained the changing face of ECEC curriculum in Switzerland:

> Twenty years ago kindergarten children were not encouraged to read because it would spoil their 'natural development as young

children'. It was not part of the curriculum. The emphasis was on play, music, drawing, theatre, oral storytelling and other forms of child development. Kindergarten is now increasingly integrated with the primary school. In some regions kindergarten is combined with first grade as the Grundstufe [basic level] which lasts three years for most children, but for quick learners just two years and for slow learners four. [Current trends in] kindergartens encourage reading along with the traditional emphases on play, music, drawing and other forms of child development.

However, these changes have not been adapted right across the country. Urs told me that a public referendum in 2012 held in the Canton of Zurich on a proposal to implement the Grundstufe plan, which had been piloted in several towns, was defeated, leaving intact the separation between kindergarten and first grade.

Teaching and taking care of young children is clearly considered to be women's work. When young men in Switzerland first consider that they might enjoy working with children, they typically put it out of their heads. Crossing the gender boundary is simply too intimidating. A recent study conducted at the Pädagogische Hochschule in Zürich reported on how few young men choose women's work of any kind. Those who have an inclination to do so bury the desire and go into another field. It is only years later that they are able to reconsider the option (Bieri Buschor *et al.*, 2012). This profile makes Benny's story even more remarkable than might first appear. With such overriding gender stereotypes in place in Swiss society, it is no wonder that a young man like Benny waited until he had reached a stage of occupational maturity before making his move to work with young children. Although he did not say he wanted to teach children earlier on, he spoke about his youth work in the church, and his second career decision to move into teaching. As a mature adult, Benny was able to cross the gender boundary with determination to succeed as a teacher of young children. The schools in Basel and the Jewish kindergarten accepted him with open arms, an indication that liberal elements in the society are important influences too (Duemmler *et al.*, 2010). Having negotiated between these two worlds of influence, Benny knows himself well enough to stay on keel, no matter how choppy the waters, as he continues to educate young children and satisfy the child within him.

Chapter 4

Elton Kikuta

Kindergarten Teacher, Jefferson Elementary School
Corvallis, Oregon, USA

'Nurturing, just not very motherly'

Elton's 27-year career as a public school teacher has always been with young children, although his training would have predicted a different trajectory. Initially enrolled in a university forestry programme at Oregon State University (OSU), Elton found himself headed towards unemployment as this sector of the economy had plummeted. Always strategic in his decision-making, he listened to his friends' suggestions that he train to be a maths teacher, which would allow him to integrate his passion for baseball coaching with an income-producing profession in a junior high school.

The training track of kindergarten to grade 8 led him unexpectedly to a student teaching placement in a kindergarten class, an experience that he was surprised to find he enjoyed. This was followed by a placement in a first-grade class in the Jefferson School in Corvallis, Oregon. Pragmatically, he accepted the placement although he had hoped and expected to be in a higher grade where he could utilize his coaching skills and conform to the career norms of his Japanese–American parents and their friends.

The first-grade placement was nonetheless fortuitous, as it led to an offer to teach in the same school in a half-day kindergarten class. Landing this job was quite an accomplishment, as the employment situation for teachers in 1984 in Oregon was pretty bleak. That year the district hired 55 teachers out of 500 applicants, and his status as a 'new hire' added even more prestige to his job. He fell into the kindergarten job unintentionally. In line with his friends' advice, he was actively pursuing work as a baseball coach and maths teacher in a junior high setting. Though he was offered work that met these criteria in a small town 'out in the country', he chose the job with the younger children for several reasons. He wanted to remain in Corvallis near the university so he could pursue a master's programme. The kindergarten job was part-time, which would allow him to invest himself in his new job and learn the ropes as a novice. In addition, he recalled his student placement: 'I remembered my experience as a first-grade teacher at Jefferson [School]. I'd enjoyed working with younger kids, and I just thought I would enjoy [the kindergarteners] as well.'

Although this decision altered his career plans to integrate sports and teaching, he decided to make the best of it. After a year in the part-time kindergarten, he was offered a full-time first-grade position, where he remained for 16 years. He was then transferred to a double-session kindergarten position that opened in his school. As Elton told me emphatically, 'So kind of by default, I ended up in kindergarten, but ended up enjoying it.' At the time of the interview, he had been 'enjoying it' for ten years.

Elton's decision to teach young children was driven not only by circumstances but also by a belief that he could give kindergarteners and first-graders an excellent education. Choosing to work in elementary school, let alone in kindergarten and first grade, was a lonely act. Friends were hardly supportive during his college years. As Elton remarked:

> While they were taking engineering courses I was taking courses on child psychology and that type of thing. And they thought it was, I guess, kind of feminine ... That was 27 years ago, I don't think there were a whole lot of men in the primary grades. And so I got teased quite a bit. But it really didn't bother me because they were my friends and I think they knew that I liked what I was doing.

Despite their reservation, his family was somewhat more supportive than his friends. Elton's parents ran a very traditional Japanese–American household with clearly defined gender roles. In such a context, a man working with young children was viewed as an anomaly. When Elton told his parents that he had taken a job as a kindergarten teacher, they thought it was 'cute'. His parents thought that salary was pegged to the age of the students, so they wondered why Elton had chosen what they thought was the lowest-paying job in the entire school system. In the end they supported his decision, although they were surprised that he stayed with the profession for such a long time. He was pleased that his family came to accept his professional choice. 'I think they know that's kind of my niche right now, and that I'm happy with it.'

Teaching style

Elton's gender minority position in his elementary education classes at the university worked to his advantage. Looking at the practical side, he found that being alone or with one other man in a group of women prepared him for his future as a male minority in the schools. He claimed that all of his professors were interested in the unique contribution to teaching that is male:

As a male you probably bring into the classroom and into the programme unique traits, and I don't know if that has to do with demeanour, if it has to do with the way you talk, the words you choose, or you just bring a certain set of, I don't know what they would be called ... I felt I was very appreciated in all the classes I took.

Teaching kindergarten in a public school that follows district- and state-wide standards creates dilemmas for early childhood educators, most of whom believe that children learn through play and that formal teaching is best left to the elementary grades. Elton's training in K–8 gives him a rather academic perspective on his work. The discourse of standards and academic achievement is the water in which he swims. So he comfortably negotiates the requirements of the district to teach pre-reading and maths as his principal endeavour. Elton feels constrained in his mission by the double-session structure, meaning that every day he teaches two groups, each for three hours. This tight schedule leaves very little time for play of any kind, as his day is divided into blocks of time labelled 'literacy, maths, handwriting and seatwork'. Twice a week, he allows the children free play time for 20 minutes.

Despite this rigid framework, Elton maintains a high level of personal interaction with the children, a relationship laced with humour, caring and challenge. Discipline is important to 'Mr K', as the children call him; and he has built his reputation not only in the Jefferson School but throughout the district as running a rather tight ship. His self-presentation features a tough outer crust with an easily accessed, soft underbelly. His primary goal is that the children should enjoy school, and he achieves this through an approach that stresses both challenge and achievement. His daily activities in the classroom ensure that every child succeeds, encouraging those who finish quickly to mentor their peers. He pushes the children to take risks, while building a safety net of group trust and compassion that mitigate failure. He encourages independence by teaching learning skills that wean students from dependence on the teacher. These principles woven together create a relaxed but dynamic learning environment that provides space for each child to find her own path through three hours of highly regimented activities. Looking at a day in Mr K's class sheds light on his unique teaching style.

A morning in Mr K's class

On the morning of my visit to his class, I was impressed by the orderliness of the routines of learning in the classroom. As the children were dropped off by their parents, they entered the class, greeted Mr K, took a worksheet from a basket, sat at an assigned place at a table, and worked at the task. In order to complete it, they relied on their own understanding, help from a friend, or directions from Mr K. According to Elton, this task helps them focus and get organized for the day.

Later in the morning after other activities, they returned to their seats at the tables for a language arts lesson about using and punctuating strong words. The children were all emergent readers. Some were able to write their own sentences while others preferred to dictate to Elton, who wrote their words on a slip of paper for them to copy. The first half hour of the lesson consisted of frontal instruction. His formal teaching engaged the children in considering the difference between 'regular words' and 'strong words'. He encouraged them to give examples, which he inserted into humorous stories about himself. Every child worked on task, as Elton conducted the lesson from his teacher space by the board. His instructions were delivered with razor-sharp precision and all of his interaction during this period was instrumental.

However, when it was time for the children to apply their new understanding by creating their own sentences, Elton moved into the children's space, leaning over to look at each child who wanted to dictate. These dyadic interactions were genuine, and Elton's intense interest in each child's thoughts came to the fore as he read their sentences aloud with much affect and flourish. As the process continued, more children became involved and requested his attention by tapping on his arm or torso. One girl wrapped her hand around his arm, waiting for her turn. Elton uses the term 'family' to describe his class, and he conducted this lesson with empathy and undivided attention in a parental manner. By the end of the activity, he managed to engage every child in the assignment at hand. All the children completed the task, but not at the same time. As the group moved to the carpet for a story, those who hadn't finished their work continued independently through completion. In this regimented environment, Elton provided space for individual expression and pacing.

Encouraging children to take risks is a central tenet of Elton's teaching. He explained to me that he believes in scaffolding children's ability to stand before the group and talk, to try out their ideas as in the writing activity described above. Elton has created a safe environment for self-expression by modelling for the children attentive listening. And he wants his students to show compassion. This process is beautifully exemplified in a show and tell activity that preceded his third story reading for the day. Arriving late due to a medical test, Paul and his mother were greeted by

Elton, who left his usual space in front of the whiteboard to approach them. Although I was too far away to overhear the conversation, it was clear to me as an objective observer that Elton listened intently to their story about the morning's events. Paul brought with him an ultrasound picture of his inner organs, and Elton invited him to show it to the group later in the day. Elton then brought Paul up to speed on the writing task. At group time on the carpet, Elton invited Paul to come forward to tell the others about his experience. By asking questions, and explaining further what Paul wanted to talk about, Elton provided group recognition of the boy's unusual and perhaps frightening morning. Elton sat in an adult-sized chair before the group, and Paul stood beside him holding his ultrasound image. Questioning him about the experience, Elton made certain that Paul himself understood what had happened, before he told his story to the rest of the group. Elton did not invite the children to ask questions but he made sure that Paul had told everything he wanted to say before bringing this episode to a close. Elton delivers a message of intense interest and compassion within the psychological safety of the group setting.

A third activity illustrates his teaching style, which encourages independence and leadership among the children. Elton prepared a worksheet enabling each student to produce their own model of the upper and lower jaws featuring the different kinds of teeth. The execution of this task required extreme precision in cutting and gluing. With great patience, Elton explained each of the many steps, one at a time, making sure that most children had completed each task before moving on. The early completers were assigned to help their friends, thus extending his teaching.

Elton stood in front of the board while giving each instruction, then moved into the children's table space to provide individual help. He constantly praised accurate work in an endless stream of matter-of-fact comments related to task execution. After most children had completed their task, Elton told them 'It's kind of fun to play with these models, but we kind of want to listen now.' Verbally recognizing the children's need to learn through play, he returned them to the task at hand to formally teach about the four types of teeth humans have. His unfailing concern for each individual's progress, as well as his recognition that the group needed to move forward, communicated care and nurturance. A few admiring girls responded to his positive approach with occasional spontaneous hugs around his waist. In this activity Elton capitalized on the need of the 5-year-old to engage in industry, while dispelling any possible feelings of inferiority. The psychologist Eric Erikson explained this developmental need of children at this age to engage in product-oriented tasks in order construct a positive self-image (1950).

Elton seems to have an intuitive grasp of this theory, which comes to the fore throughout the working day in his classroom.

Emotion and nurturance

Outward emotional expression seems remote to Elton's normal manner of interacting. He explained that his Japanese parents were not emotional people, and his father particularly exhibited little affect. In our interview, he spoke of nurturing by explaining his adjustment to working in the kindergarten in his first job:

> My expectations were too high, both behaviourally and academically. My pacing was too fast, but I was able to make some adjustments. I had a lot of guidance. I don't want to stereotype kindergarten teachers, but the ones I worked with were very nurturing, I wouldn't say they were older but they were just very motherly, and I believe they kind of took me under their wing. I guess I consider myself nurturing, but just not very motherly. My styling here is pretty direct, and so with all that mothering and nurturing it taught me to tone down my expectations and my pace and I feel comfortable with the age now, I really enjoy the age now. And well I guess that's how I got into kindergarten.

In this reflective statement, Elton indicates that teaching young children has enabled him to find and develop his ability to nurture his students through his day-to-day interactions. He believes that he must earn their respect through significant one-on-one contact. He accomplishes this through humour, finding the 'inside joke' that works for each child in his class, and this creates closeness with individual children. He claims that he is 'big on proximity,' while his explanation touches on emotional rather than physical closeness. He communicates his respect for the children, expecting that they in turn will respect him and their classmates because they know that he truly cares about them on a personal and individual level. 'I let them know that I like being here, [that] this is my number one choice, and that we're like a family.'

Another expression of caring is his use of body language. 'I'll lean in to talk to a child, whisper to them. And I think that provides, you know, a bit of intimacy as far as making a connection with that child.' I observed this strategy frequently during the formal lessons, particularly during the times Elton moved from his teacher space by the board into the children's territory at the tables. Time after time, he 'leaned in' to hear their question or make a suggestion about accomplishing the assignment. The interactions were largely instrumental and task-oriented, but the quality of these formal learning dialogues provided the basis of Elton's nurturing attitude towards his students.

Elton was more likely to be the recipient than the initiator of physical gestures of affection from both current and former students. I observed occasional instances of children hugging him, and he responded with gentle acceptance of the affection. Although I did not observe his returning these hugs, he claims that he does respond in kind: 'Well I try to hug them back, and if they hang on too long I trip [laughs]. So I guess it's a compliment, I take it as a compliment.' Thus physical contact with the children, particularly girls, is part of his repertoire, although it is not a major theme in his teaching style.

Compassion is a goal for Elton, and this sometimes takes physical form in turns of giving and receiving affection. Elton related an incident of his exhibiting particularly 'scary' behaviour towards his class when they misbehaved at a school assembly. Afterwards, a girl in his class approached him, kissed him on the cheek and then sat down. Later when he asked her what the kiss was about, she responded empathetically: 'It just seemed like you needed a little kiss right then, that's what my mom does to me.' It appears that the compassion Elton has nurtured among his students can be turned towards him as a member of the classroom community that he has worked so hard to create.

Masculinity and professional identity

Elton's professional gender identity posits a duality between the male and female, as archetypal characteristics not only in the educational setting but also in families. Perhaps the basis of this bifurcation of gender roles is his conception of his own family's Japanese culture, in which 'the dad goes to work and he's the disciplinarian and the mom does all the nurturing'. He finds expression of his own masculinity in his strict disciplinary style, which he calls 'running a tight ship'. His discipline consists of clear instructions, boundaries, positive reinforcement and humour, all of which contribute to the children's clear desire to cooperate and behave within the classroom norms he has set. He has earned a reputation in the Corvallis School District as a no-nonsense teacher who knows how to manage the behaviour of his students, particularly that of rambunctious little boys.

Elton characterizes the masculine teaching style in three ways: by his demeanour, language and norms or expectations. By demeanour, he means a 'direct style', saying and doing what you mean with no emotional cover-up: 'We do a lot of things kind of regimented.' By language, he means precision with explanations and directions, as well as speaking loudly. By norms and expectations, he means his ability to communicate high-performance expectations, which include academic, social and emotional domains. He believes that men in the classroom have a distinct advantage over women in the realm of discipline because of the male role model that they portray: 'For the most part, behaviour management may be a little easier for a man in the classroom, because it's part of the old "wait till your dad gets home" thing, and the dad's right here.' This advantage comes to the fore especially with students from traditional family structures where 'the dad of the house is the guy that you don't want to get mad, because you know he's the one with the heavy hand'.

Another aspect of his masculinity is Elton's passion for sports. The rhetoric and symbols of sports permeate his speech and even find expression on the walls of his classroom. I was struck by the stereotypical male feeling expressed in the physical appearance of the classroom: football team paraphernalia, sparse decorations, a dearth of children's creative art work and an orderly arrangement of the tools of teaching. He refers to his use of a whistle on field trips as a metaphor for coaching a sports team. His desire for children to take a degree of risk is also the language of sports. He enjoys talking about football and other sports with the children in his class, and his unswerving support for the local university's teams fits with his OSU lanyard, which he wears prominently around his neck to hold his school ID badge. Children's spontaneous drawings related to the local sports comprise part of the wall decorations. He views himself as a male role model for both boys and girls in his class. He portrays a father image as the authority. However, another important feature of the male role model he characterizes is his challenge to the stereotyped male. 'They can see that a man can be nurturing, can work with young kids.'

As a family man Elton is well aware of the father role from up close. He has two children from his former marriage, and currently shares the parenting of his girlfriend's children. He distinguishes between the emotional content of a father's and a teacher's role in his response to my question about caution in touching children:

> Showing affection towards children is not a concern. It's because I think even though I'm a dad and everything, I would touch my kids differently, or hug my kids differently than I would hug a kindergartner in my class. So I guess with my kids I would hold them in my lap ... Kids this age, they still like to kiss, and so I would let them know that kissing's for home.

His comment illustrates his physical warmth both as a father and as a teacher, and the boundaries that he sets for himself and for the children regarding touch.

Elton's well-articulated masculine self-image is balanced by feminine traits as well. He explains this softer side of his teaching style by positively referring to those aspects of nurturing that he has included in his professional identity. At the beginning of his teaching career, he found being around 5-year-olds 'a little strange, [because] I didn't have any younger brothers or sisters'. The rhetoric of family is central to his professional self-identity. For example, he perceives that children view him in a parental role: 'I guess they kind of still see me as their father figure too, although I do get called mom quite a bit.' Over the years, he found his special way with young children and developed his own sense of nurturing, which is strongly related to modifying his expectation for success according to the needs of individual children. 'I feel everybody needs the same chance, the same opportunities to succeed, and that may look different for different kids.' He strives to help children feel comfortable to take risks in the knowledge that they are safe. He described this approach in the following quote:

> I'm not a hoverer. I really try to teach the kids what they need to do and let them do it instead of doing it for them. I want the kids to feel safe in here but I also want them to … take a risk if it's a true risk, whether it's spelling a word or going up and talking in front of the class.

Elton expresses his nurturance by creating a safe environment that is always challenging. He wants the children to take risks, knowing that they have a safety net to fall back into.

Contrasting his own masculinity with that of other male teachers helps him define his own professional gender identity. In our interview he remarked more than once about the spartan appearance of his classroom walls. He noted that a school supervisor was initially bothered by the lack of appropriate classroom decorations, a phenomenon that Elton disparagingly calls 'cutesy' remarking that there are lots of men who are 'artsy and craftsy … but I'm not one of them'. Here Elton emphasizes his masculinity, drawing a line between himself and other men whom he views as perhaps effeminate.

Maintaining his own traditional masculinity while allowing for a softer and more nurturing side, he selects his work wardrobe to reflect both aspects. He often wears pink or purple dress shirts, which challenge the male stereotyped clothing palette, yet maintain the conventional male dress code of a shirt that buttons down the front. On the day of my visit he was wearing a white shirt with a tie featuring teddy bears, a combination that integrates the serious male image with a more nurturing message. For Elton, his sartorial presentation marks the tension between the dual identities of a man in a nurturing role.

Broader cultural context: the case of Oregon

In order to achieve a broader perspective on the immediate cultural context of Elton's work, I interviewed Denise Gorthy, the principal of Jefferson School in Corvallis, and Will Parnell, who is the pedagogical director of the flagship laboratory childcare centre and coordinates the Master's in Early Childhood Education Program at Portland State University.

Will brought a fine-tuned geographical perspective to the question of men's acceptance in the profession. He claims that in liberal pockets, such as downtown Portland and on the university campus, there is widespread support for men working with young children. This liberal outlook is reflected in a general acceptance of alternative lifestyles in the Portland area, an openness that Will refers to as 'keep it weird'. A case in point, according to Will, is the current school superintendent who is a self-proclaimed lesbian. But just a few miles out of town in the suburbs, the conservative influence predicates against including men in the ECEC workforce. This conservative viewpoint is encouraged by the general religious atmosphere in Oregon, which claims the nation's highest rate of 'obscure churches' (see, for example, Johnson, 1963; Schmitt, 1952). Will defines these churches as being on the fringe of Christianity, and exerting significant 'influence on their members about those traditional ways of thinking and those traditional models of who should be taking care of the young children'. This influence is in the direction of supporting traditional gender roles in the early childhood classroom. When he looked for a job with young children after completing a master's degree, Will was bluntly rejected by day care directors and school principals in the Portland suburbs, but finally landed a job in the city. He noted a liberal tendency regarding the socio-cultural atmosphere in Corvallis, as evidenced by the town's support for gay rights in an electoral referendum, a vote matching results in Portland. He attributed this liberal outlook to the 'university atmosphere'. Corvallis is a typical university town with a permanent population of 55,000 and a transient student population of 20,000.

Denise confirmed Will's description of the openness found in Corvallis. She supports gender balance in the school for a number of reasons. Firstly, she thinks that children from single-parent families, of whom there are some in her school, benefit from interacting with a man on a daily basis given that there is no constant male figure at home. Secondly, men 'bring a different perspective' … without getting 'wrapped up in all of the touchy feely things'. She also notes that men's voices 'cut across the din of the classroom and children hear what they're being asked to do'. Because of her belief in the advantages of a balance of men and women teachers, Denise seeks job applications from men when she has an opening. Male applicants for elementary teaching positions are not nearly as plentiful as female applicants. One source of applicants is the student teachers who work at Jefferson. If they are competent, she encourages them to submit a résumé so that she can weigh their merits among the applicant pool.

Despite these generally positive attitudes towards inclusion of men in the early childhood workforce, Denise noted caution about men touching young children in the school context, and Will described this as a 'troubling issue'. Denise told me:

> We try to be careful in terms of how much we touch children and hug them, or even put our hands on them, and I know … my male teachers are hyper-aware of those kinds of things, and are especially careful in terms of where they might place their hands to help a child. They also make sure doors are open and they are not alone with children, to avoid any suspicions.

Over Elton's 27 years of employment at the school, Denise has not heard a single complaint related to his gender, nor has she sensed hesitation from parents about placing their children in his class. To the contrary, she has found that parents often request that their child be placed in his class for positive reasons, including his reputation as an effective disciplinarian.

Despite the relatively liberal attitude towards men childcare workers in Portland, Will has witnessed an anti-male bias from time to time, even in his own school. For example, a young girl told her parents that a male caregiver 'licked his finger before pushing back a tuft of her hair'. The parents registered a complaint, demanding to know why Will was not watching this teacher during naptime. Will reflected on the deep-seated suspicion that men teachers are potential child molesters:

> And so I think unfortunately, even for me, with men, there's this divide that happens, and I think it's so engrained in us, like, men are going to do these things to children … It's out there in the media and it's out there in so much of the world, so … then there's this question of why does a man ultimately go into this field, what is his desire or drive?

Both Will and Denise have managed to recruit men in teaching jobs in their institutions. In Will's centre 10 per cent of the staff are men. Denise has 6 men working in her school out of a total staff of 41. The Oregon work environment is driven by the high-tech industry – what Will calls the 'silicon forest' in and around Portland. He claims that well-paid jobs in high tech compete with lower-paying jobs in education and that men tend to gravitate towards these more lucrative professions, as the culture pressures them to fill the role of family breadwinner. In the following excerpt from his interview, he tried to explain the reluctance of men to consider jobs in ECEC:

> So if you follow that structured model of young men who are supposed to get married, have a family, and a career to support the family, which to me seems to be outdated and so outmoded, it's not even, I don't even think it's a part of our reality anymore, but it's a part of our thinking. It's part of the way we live nowadays … So many men are not going to choose early childhood as the way to make the money for their family, and maybe that does come back to some of the realities.

The salary structure of the non-profit day care centre prevents both men and women from staying in the job for very long. However, Will brought a contrary example of a young man on his staff who is totally committed to working with young children. This teacher has just married and does not yet have children to support, so he can currently afford to work in a relatively low-pay job. One solution is for the men to move on to administrative level positions, which both Will and Denise have seen happen among the men teachers. The public school system in Corvallis has a higher pay scale than Will's day care centre, and the salary incentives there permit men to remain in the classroom. During his 27 years of teaching, Elton has never desired to leave the classroom. He may be considered an exception to the usual trajectory of men moving up the career ladder by leaving the classroom.

The cultural matrix

Elton's decision to work with young children was influenced by his actively pursuing an acceptable male career track in teaching. Although he signed up for a university programme leading to licensing in grades K–8 (ages 5–13), he initially intended to work at the upper limit of this age range, doing what men are supposed to do: teach maths and coach baseball. His acquiescence to a kindergarten student teacher placement was driven by his practical desire to navigate the system and complete his degree and teaching licence. A second placement in a first-grade class was simply another hurdle to get over before achieving his original career goal. Upon graduation, he only sought teaching positions according to his initial plan, and was offered such a job in a small town far out of the city, which he turned down in favour of an offer to teach kindergarten at the Jefferson School where he had done his student teaching. This choice was made not out of a commitment to work with young children, but as a practical step to locating himself near the university so that he could enrol in a graduate programme.

His parents were not keen about the kindergarten placement. But in a tight job market, they gave a nodding approval. After all, he would be working for the public schools, and there is plenty of mobility within the system. Calling his job 'cute' may be seen as disapproval or disappointment, and may indicate that his choice might not bring honour to the family. The culture of cute (kawaii) is currently widespread in Japan, and may be the source of Elton's reference to his parents' response to his career choice. Professor Hiroto Murasawa, an expert on the culture of beauty at Osaka Shoin Women's University, believes cute is 'a mentality that breeds non-assertion,' and ascribes the use of the term to the notion that 'individuals who choose to stand out get beaten down' (Kageyama, 2006). Japanese culture places family honour as a central value, and the careers of the children may be seen as enhancing or detracting from that honour. It is possible that their status as an immigrant family attenuated the parents' influence on their son's career choice. The bottom line is that Elton made his own decision.

Another factor that might have enabled Elton to go ahead with kindergarten teaching is the academicization over the past 30 years of American public school kindergartens (Marcon, 2012). There has been pressure on public school districts to emphasize such academic topics as reading and maths in the kindergartens at the expense of play. Thus the model that Elton saw in the schools was an academic model of formal learning. This model dovetailed with his image of how teachers teach and how children learn. Trained to teach junior high school with formal lessons, Elton was able to adapt this paradigm of teaching in the kindergarten with a level of comfort. Thus choosing to teach kindergarten might have fitted snugly with his own conceptions of how a man teaches, be it kindergarten or junior high school. The daily garb of button-down shirts and necktie feeds into this masculine model of teaching. Tying the whole package together, the Japanese cultural expectations of doing a man's work, plus the formal teaching supported by the public schools in Corvallis, allowed Elton to resolve the dissonance between his view of his own masculinity and the job offer of teaching kindergarten.

As Elton embarked on his career as a teacher of young children, he found that 5- and 6-year-old children have their own emotional and social needs, which are expressed as affection, frustration, fear and anger. Being the sensitive person he is, Elton was able to adjust his teaching style to the needs of his students. Although he maintains formal aspects of the frontal teacher, he also demonstrates a softer side that emphasizes caring, nurturing and concern, as exhibited through his careful and well-articulated explanations and instructions. Another mode of nurturing is a relaxed time frame, which allows for individual differences in completing the structured tasks that speak to the formalized language arts and maths curriculum. His teaching is systematic, but his tenor is human and down to earth.

Elton does not sit on the floor with the children, but he does lean over and look at the child eye to eye, face to face. He is courteous and sincere, and takes each child entirely seriously. His masculinity takes the shape of the caring father who supports each child so he can succeed. This individual emphasis may emanate from Japanese family life, in which the mother educates each child individually, guiding, prompting, supporting and encouraging – one on one (Yamamoto *et al.*, 2006). If this is the role of the Japanese mother, then we might ask: How did Elton adapt this cross-gender modelling? He explained that his father was largely absent during his upbringing and that he was raised by his mother. Perhaps this strong modelling affected his view of teaching and learning.

Thus we can see in Elton a by-product of American masculine culture, traditional Japanese values and a school system that favours academic learning for young children. The interaction of these forces has resulted in the crystallization of Elton's unique teaching style. Furthermore, the economic forces in play at the critical moments in Elton's career led him to choose work with young children as a lifelong endeavour, much to the good fortune of Corvallis children for over a quarter of a century.

Chapter 5

Levien Nieuwenhuis

Kindergarten Teacher, Montessori School
Zeist, the Netherlands

'I like it, but it was not my dream in the beginning'

As I looked up from my camera in a corner of the Montessori kindergarten room, my attention was grabbed by the sudden image of Levien, sporting an impish smile, cruising across the room on a scooter that one of the children had brought to school. Keeping track of him throughout the morning proved challenging as he moved quietly and deliberately from activity to activity, from child to child. Although the walls of his classroom are not richly decorated with teacher-made materials or the children's creative work, Levien's charismatic presence fills the space. If you asked him six years ago to predict where he might be on this day at age 30, he probably would have described a junior high classroom of young adolescents studying Dutch history. But as opportunities presented themselves and as he discovered his own proclivity for working with young children, Levien manoeuvred his way into this kindergarten teaching job as nimbly as he glided across the classroom on the scooter.

After high school Levien set his sights on becoming a physiotherapist. Without much planning or preparation he enrolled on a four-year training programme. Although the studies were not difficult, he was alienated by the practical examinations, which required drawing the human musculature and bone structure. After a year he abandoned this career direction, and found himself once again searching for a profession. His friends suggested that he drop by the open house at the local Hogeschool (institute of higher education) to see if teaching might interest him. He agreed without enthusiasm and paid a visit to the Hogeschool in Utrecht, near his hometown. This in turn led to a tepid decision to pursue a teacher training course. Levien described his change of direction candidly:

> I went to the Montessori programme first and I said, 'Oh it's ok', and when I started it was not that I wanted to be a teacher at that moment. Maybe it was already in me, but at that moment it wasn't that I wanted to be a teacher for sure. It was [rather that] I had a bad study year [in physiotherapy] and I wanted to do something that I like – that I think is nice.

In retrospect he views his decision positively: 'And then I did it and yeah, I'm glad that I did it.' He indeed chose to specialize in Montessori education, which turned out to be a prescient move leading to his current successful five-year career as a kindergarten teacher.

His family supported his decision:

> Well my parents said, 'If you are happy, it's ok. The best way to do
> your job is that you are happy about it, because you will keep on
> doing it longer.' And now I was happy about my studies and when
> I finished I was happy about teaching.

His male friends were less supportive, pointing to the low salaries teachers earned. One younger friend compared himself to Levien: 'I have a big salary and I'm just starting.' Levien's retort indicates his own convictions: 'And I said, "I know, but you don't have to [choose a career] for the money".' Levien critically views his friend's financial lens as very masculine and totally irrelevant to his own values. 'I think this is the best place for me, and the money comes in second.' At the time of the interview he assessed his financial needs as a single man to be adequately met by his kindergarten teacher's salary. His plans for the future when he will have a family to support include moving into a school management position that is better remunerated than classroom teaching.

Socially he found the academic programme at the Hogeschool to be rather isolating. In his first year there were 3 other men among 50 women. In the second year his male colleagues dropped out, leaving him as the only man in the entire group. However, he did connect with one woman in the programme through their morning bicycle ride to the college, and with others during their cafeteria study breaks. By the third year, another man joined the programme, and they became a 'duo', studying and working together on school-related tasks as much as possible. 'When we were sick of class we'd go into town for a beer together and that kind of thing. That was nice, but it slowed me down.'

The Montessori training focuses on a range of age groups. Within this framework he decided to specialize in three age groups during his training, which qualified him to teach ages 6 to 12 in the public schools. It took him an extra year to complete the programme, but he later learned that a five-year course of study is considered advantageous by some of the school managers (the literal translation of the Dutch word for school principals).

In his final year of study he was placed in a suburban Montessori school in the nearby upper-middle-class suburban town of Zeist, where he was assigned to a higher grade. The school manager was pleased with his work, and when he graduated she asked him to fill in for teachers who were absent. A job unexpectedly opened up at kindergarten level, and she offered it to him. Levien reflected on his decision to accept the offer:

> When I was placed in the kindergarten, I said, 'Ooh that was not what I expected.' Then again, it's nice. I started to learn the benefits and the positive sides to it, and now I'm a kindergarten teacher for five years.

As he looked back, he concluded, 'I like it, but it was not my dream in the beginning to do it'.

Levien claimed that he has learned a great deal on the job about working with young children, and perhaps his most important conclusion is the value of play: 'Playing is also learning and that's what I learned, and that's what I'm comfortable to do now.' The Montessori programme is structured around playful tasks that the children choose and carry out mostly individually and sometimes in pairs. In his class, he has created an atmosphere of independent work and play in a relaxed atmosphere that engages the children in self-selected activities. During my visit to his class, I observed only two incidences of his intervening in children's decision-making by guiding them to choose a particular activity. While most of the children carried out their task at their own desk or on a small movable carpet on the floor, some selected open-ended play venues such as the sand table, the doll corner, or the Lego table in the common area in the hallway. Levien focused his energies on supporting children's thinking by listening and asking challenging questions. His mediating activities centred on structured play tasks such as seriation puzzles, producing numbers with rubber stamps, and copying a printed design using a small building toy. During those extended interactions, he intently engaged each child in discussion about what she accomplished, and extended her thinking further by offering thought-provoking questions and additional challenges using the same material. The extremely personal nature of these conversations and their quiet tone made it difficult for me to pick up on their content; however, as an experienced observer and former kindergarten teacher, I was impressed by the intellectual excitement Levien generated. Of all aspects of his teaching, Levien especially enjoys his work with individuals, which he feels supports their cognitive growth:

> I like when children are going to read or something and I help them to go further beyond their educational level. For example in mathematics they learn how to count and then they learn how

to skip count. That's what I like, yeah, especially the individual attention, to help a child on his own level – that's what I most enjoy.

He also gains pleasure from seeing the children happy as a result of their learning. For example, when asked to state his greatest accomplishment as a teacher, he told me about a Polish child who came to his class without speaking a word of Dutch:

> This was about a child who is going on 4 and doesn't speak any common language [with me or with the children in the class]. I had to figure out how to communicate with her, how to start contact. When I compare her then with how she is now, she's talking a lot to me, she's coming a lot to me, and she's very happy. I think that's the most special thing to see.

Later he commented that the child's learning can mostly be attributed to her own initiative; however, he also took a great deal of pride in this accomplishment, recognizing the significance of his contribution to her language growth.

I was charmed by Levien's direct style of interaction, which is both personal and personable. When deciding where to focus his energies, he carefully observed the quality of the work/play activities in the classroom, and approached individual children whom he thought would benefit from his intervention. He then based his interactions on the Montessori philosophy of scaffolding independence: 'We help you to do it, if you can't do it on your own.' He continued by explaining that in such cases his task is to help the child achieve independence by learning how to work independently.

Levien offered me a stool for sitting during my morning's observation. When I saw how he used his own stool, I understood his concern for my comfort and appreciated his practical solution. He occupied himself throughout the entire free play time by focusing on different children who could benefit from his mediation. His stool seemed to be an appendage of his body, as he carried it with him from child to child, seated himself next to the child with whom he chose to work, and made eye contact as well as a physical gesture which included a pat on the shoulder or a light touch on the wrist. He intervened in such a way that the children continued their activity while he watched up close and spoke with them. In some cases he helped them directly, but mostly he asked, explained, demonstrated and inspired. There is no absolute standard that he expected to attain: rather, he helped the children measure themselves against their own performance and then go beyond. Empathy was the foundation of these interactions, both cognitively and emotionally. On the cognitive level, Levien tuned into the child's understanding and sense of wonder. On the emotional level, he shared their frustrations as well as their joy in finally achieving the task at hand. Levien invested himself in each dialogue, taking pleasure in understanding what the child had already done, as he supported that child's persistence in working towards the chosen goal.

I noticed that Levien's mediation was not limited to the free play session in his classroom. It extended to the outdoor recess and other school activities beyond the classroom walls. Three examples illustrate his unique style of intensive one-on-one interaction: in the classroom, on the playground and in the school gymnasium. Each vignette features one particular child, which highlights Levien's pedagogical disposition to concentrate on the individual.

Tineke

As I have shown, Levien focused on each child through engagement in self-chosen tasks. A classic Montessori exercise involves learning how to tie shoes using a lacing board. Tineke had chosen this task and was working at her desk as Levien approached with his stool in hand. He sat next to her, speaking with her about her failed attempts to tie the required knots. She explained to Levien what she had done, and showed him how she approached the challenge, expressing frustration that the knot she made did not hold. Levien reached his arms around Tineke, cradling her from each side, as he patiently demonstrated how to tie the knot. Then he suggested that she imitate these actions, which she did as he silently observed from the side. With each failure on Tineke's part, Levien again showed her the correct way to tie the knot, and once again suggested that she try it out for herself. After three rounds of teacher demonstration and Tineke's failed attempts, he left her to continue working on her own. Half an hour later he returned, once again encircling her with his outstretched arms, and again modelled the desired movements with the laces. He noticed that her attempts were becoming more accurate, and continued to encourage her. This time, Tineke succeeded in her second try and clapped excitedly as Levien enthusiastically shared her accomplishment. I found myself rooting for Tineke to tie the knot, and when she succeeded I was as thrilled as she and Levien were with her triumph. Having confirmed her new expertise, Levien marked in Tineke's journal that she had successfully tied the knot. With a gentle pat on her shoulder and a few words of praise, he moved on to another child, stool in hand.

Sandrien

I was drawn to a second example of Levien's caring style of mediation during a photo session for school pictures. While at first dismayed that I had scheduled my visit on the day of school picture taking, I was amply rewarded with an unexpected exposure to Levien's clownish side, which I might not have seen on a regular school day. When Levien was told that it was his turn to bring the children to the gym for pictures, he gently raised his voice, and immediately everyone quietened down. He explained about the transition to the gym, and the children lined up politely to walk down the hall. Levien took up the rear, holding hands with one of the younger 4-year-olds. I followed behind, enjoying this 'Pied Piper of Hamelin' scene; however, in this case the piper took his place at the end of the line. Having arrived in the gym, the children arranged themselves on benches at the edge of the room and waited their turn for an individual picture session.

About ten minutes into this newly established routine, Sandrien arrived with her mother. She had sustained a slight head injury that morning, so arrived late, sporting a colourful cloth hairband that covered the wound. Both Sandrien and her mother were clearly upset by the morning trauma, and the mother spoke to Levien at length about what had occurred. After adjusting her daughter's hairband for the last time, the mother left and Sandrien sat quietly, talking with friends. Levien approached her, squatting down to her height, to discuss the morning's events at home. When it was her turn to be photographed, she expressed reluctance to take her place on the photographer's stool. Levien held her hand, and convinced her to try it out. They walked together to the seat, and he helped settle her comfortably. The photographer was dismayed at Sandrien's refusal to smile. His efforts to cajole her into a bit of laughter failed to produce the desired results. Levien promptly swung into action, positioning himself behind the photographer where Sandrien could see him. He began to jump high, swaying from side to side, clapping his hands, all in order to produce a smile. He delighted not only the girl but also the photographer and his assistant, who invited him to continue entertaining other despondent clients in such a delightful manner. Levien turned down the offer, preferring to sit next to Sandrien on the bench to cheer her up. As someone who cares deeply about the emotional lives of children, I was glued to this episode, wondering what wonderful strategy Levien would produce next, as he continued his discourse with his injured student.

Maarten

For Montessori children the playground offers a very different level of activity to the controlled, task-oriented indoor play. Like most playgrounds around the world, this sweeping space invites children to interact freely with their friends while physically challenging themselves and one another. Montessori philosophy supports collaboration between children of different ages, and the school staff purposefully arrange for children from various grades to be on the playground at the same times. A uniquely Dutch element of the playground is a small fenced enclosure for playing football. This venue is attractive to both kindergarteners and older students, evidenced by younger and older girls and boys lining up against a nearby wall to wait their turn for a match. I was interested in this venue because of its cultural uniqueness and began to video the children's play in the enclosure. I was soon drawn to the periphery of the football match, as an important drama began to unfold.

Wanting to kick the ball with his young students, Levien took his place in the queue. The game progressed and new players entered while others departed. Maarten, a particularly large boy in Levien's class, had been playing in the enclosure, but was replaced by another player. Sullen, angry, and demonstrably upset, he took his place once again by the wall, waiting for another turn. Levien moved in, wrapped his arms around his student, leaned against the wall, and hunched over to reach Maarten's eye level. Speaking softly while brushing a bit of dirt off Maarten's sleeve, Levien listened to complaints about the unfair manner in which the boy had been ejected from the enclosure. Levien gently guided him away, trying to lift Maarten over his head in a joking manner. When the child resisted, Levien set him down, and they walked on together, maintaining their intimate contact. As Maarten's anger subsided, Levien guided him around the corner out of sight of the football enclosure until they reached a chair near the door to a classroom. Here Levien helped Maarten sit down and continued to hover over the seated child as they spoke. Eventually Levien left the scene to regain his place in the waiting line for the next duo football match, while Maarten went his own way.

At the end of the day, Levien asked Maarten to read to the class a story he had mastered. When I asked Levien later about the incident, he explained his goal of helping Maarten think about what he had done, so that he could 'get on with his day'. Levien further clarified that Maarten was under stress because his family had just moved to a new home and this had deprived him of his parents' usual close attention to his needs. There was no hint of punishment in Levien's actions; rather he clearly supported Maarten in reflection aimed at fostering resilience to bounce back. During the entire ten minutes of this episode, Levien responded affectionately to the distraught child. Neither anger nor frustration had a place in their interaction. Levien summarized his own actions:

> I think he needed attention but he was asking for it in the wrong way. That's why I put him on a chair next to the door. I said to him

that he can go off if he changes his face to a happy face. But he decided to stay and grumble.

These three incidents demonstrate Levien's empathy for children as they learn cognitively, emotionally and socially. Tineke was cognitively challenged by the lace board task, Sandrien was emotionally challenged by the demand to be photographed while wearing a headband covering her wound, and Maarten was socially challenged by the exigencies of the football enclosure. Levien's charisma in dealing with all three incidents is quiet yet powerful. As he empathically helped each child find a workable solution, he empowered each to continue learning independently, according to the problem encountered.

Caring

These vignettes show that Levien was acutely tuned in to the children's emotional state, be it frustration, distress, anger or joy. His ability to deal effectively with each situation rested on his correct reading of the current reality and his empathic response. His caring attitude found expression in the manner in which he responded to each child's emotional and physical needs. Levien gave the impression of being present from his first handshake in the morning when the children arrive to the final words of departure as the last child leaves. Touching is an inherent element of the relaxed classroom milieu Levien has created. Sometimes children stroked his face, sometimes they stretched their arms around his waist, and sometimes they held his hands while dancing around him. While hugs were abundant, and I observed that they were almost always initiated by the children, particularly girls, Levien's response was affectionate tolerance and comfort, as he slipped his hand into the child's hand, or allowed them to nestle into his lap for a moment. In our interview he explained his sensibilities about showing outward affection:

> I do want to let the children know I like them, but I want to keep a distance. For example now, for me I have a lot of physical contact with the children. It's [picking] them up and, but that's the limit. Sometimes children want to give me a kiss or something and I'm not allowing that because ok I want to have a little bit of distance because you never know what kind of story will [develop].

My observations confirmed Levien's special style of playful physical interaction. During my morning in his class, I noticed him tickle and lift a child over his head before setting him down gently on his feet. However, if the child resisted, as when Maarten did in the playground incident described above, Levien desists immediately, and shifts to a less playful mode of comfort, such as holding hands. Levien made himself physically present for the children.

While helping a child with a building construction on the floor, he stretched out comfortably in a half-sitting, half-lying position. In that instance, a girl found her way into his lap and from this close proximity watched intently as Levien helped her friend with the building. Once satisfied, she scrambled away to her own self-chosen task.

I observed another type of contact that involved lifting children to a vantage point. A visually impaired child had completed a seriation task of gluing onto a paper strip pictures of different-sized balloons by order of size. When Levien sat with her to discuss the result, he realized that she had erred and perhaps misunderstood the task. Hand in hand he led her to a wall on the opposite side of the classroom, where he lifted her to stand on a toy shelf so that she could look closely at other children's completed pictures. He supported her, one hand on each side, as she inspected these works, and then set her down on the floor. He later explained to me that he only lifts children from the sides, careful not to touch the front of their body. As in the other episodes mentioned above, this kind of touching comes naturally to Levien, and is a critical part of his effective classroom work.

Levien's lap seems like a very safe place for both boys and girls. During the morning meeting at the beginning of the day, Levien raised two children to his knees, as he took his place in the circle. These children had evidenced separation difficulties with their parents on arrival that day, and Levien's response functioned as a helpful transition from home to school. He began the meeting with his two lap sitters, but quickly encouraged them to move to their own chair in the circle, signalling for them to slide down and take their own place. The ease with which Levien handled these situations results from a professional maturation process in which he has evaluated the pros and cons of close physical contact:

> I want to know that the children are happy. And if they aren't happy I will try to comfort them by sitting on my lap if they want … When children are sad they want to be comforted … sitting on my lap and the attention part. That has grown the last years, because at first I thought I was very stiff because you have to be careful as a male teacher. It wouldn't be the first time that … some sick stories have been fabricated and that a male teacher has been accused of something he didn't do. You have to watch out for stories which can affect your career as a male teacher.

Importantly, the school supports Levien's attitude towards physical contact with the children. Such a liberal policy makes it possible for Levien to function comfortably and to rely on his own sensibilities.

Levien's professional identity is characterized by a clear distinction between himself and female colleagues, particularly in the realm of caring. His self-perception in this regard is almost deprecating:

> Well for myself I thought I'm not the ultimate kindergarten teacher. I'm not, like we said with Anneke (a female colleague), I'm not that caring, I'm not that caring and protecting. (I don't ask the child), 'Oh, what's wrong with you?' In my opinion that's a real kindergarten teacher ... And I'm not like that I think. So that's why I felt ok, that it will be tough ... Although I'm not perfect, I think the interaction with the children would be hard because I'm very stingy with words, and I'm not always direct.

Another aspect of his professional self-image is his preference for children's academic learning over their emotional and social development. Levien described his internal debate when he was offered the job as kindergarten teacher:

> When children are going to read, are going to count, are going to make sums, then I find it interesting, when they are playing in the doll corner it's not my cup of tea, and that's why I was afraid that [teaching kindergarten] wasn't my thing.

Levien's claim that caring is unimportant to him clearly contradicts his behaviour, which exhibits a high level of nurturance for children throughout the day. However, his preference for the academic and cognitive aspects of the curriculum over the social and emotional was borne out during my full day's visit. On the one hand, he was keenly tuned into the children's affective side, and he responded to each child with concern and empathy. On the other hand, he stayed out of the doll corner throughout the day, except once when a child approached him with a request to open a doctor kit whose latch was stuck shut. His response here was instrumental. He opened the latch, followed the child into the doll corner, saw that she was launched in her play, and then returned to another child whose work on a cognitive task was engaging the minds of both child and teacher.

In our interview, Levien stipulated the boundaries of his caring when he spoke of tending to the children's needs in the toilet. The Montessori approach encourages independence in all realms, including toileting. Therefore, if a child wets himself, the child is expected to change his own clothing. Soiling is another story. In those cases, Levien says that he will clean up the child: 'Yeah then I do it, one time. And the next time when it happens then I call the parents [and say to them:] "OK, you can do it." I don't consider it to be the teacher's task.' His judgement in this matter is based not only on personal sensitivities but also on professional judgement, which proscribes leaving the classroom unattended for any length of time. He recalled one incident of taking a very long time to clean up a child, after which he found an extremely chaotic situation upon returning to the classroom. As he said humorously: 'In the meantime a kid was breaking down the class.'

When viewing himself professionally, Levien sees a big difference between him and his female colleagues in terms of his encouraging children to exhibit daring in their play. For example, the school faculty discussed whether or not they should permit children to climb onto the roof of a small playhouse in the playground. Levien found himself in a minority of one, pitting himself against the women in the group. Whereas he thought that children who are interested in climbing on the playhouse roof should be allowed to follow their whim, others were concerned about the children's safety:

> The playhouse is built to [have children climb on it] and if they fall they fall. Children have to fall to know their limitations. And if everything is forbidden then they don't know their limitations, and if [in the future] they accidentally ... fall, they break something because they don't know how to fall.

His arguments for allowing children to climb on the structure were well-articulated but not adequately convincing to his female colleagues, who prevailed in the final decision. This discussion left Levien feeling isolated: 'At that time I was very sorry that I was only with women.'

Levien believes that his presence as a man and his masculine approach are beneficial to the boys in his class. He thinks that he understands them better than a woman could, and that he appreciates their particular style of rough-and-tumble play:

> I think they can be themselves. If they want to struggle or something, ok, I let them. It has to be in a nice way ... I look at it individually ... I know they can play a little bit physically and if it goes well, so I allow them. So I look at the kid and then I decide if I allow it or not, based on the fact that I know what they are capable of [doing].

Levien wears his masculinity on his sleeve. Despite his bounteous nurturing in both a physical and a psychological sense, he maintains a relaxed masculine profile tempered by his deep care and concern for the children. On the day of my visit, he wore jeans and a brightly coloured T-shirt imprinted with a picture of 'the pissing necklace'. This shirt symbolically refers to the real pissing necklace that is donned by the child who leaves the classroom to go down the hall to the toilets. This kindergarten humour represents the tension between a female accoutrement, the necklace, while maintaining a traditionally masculine appearance. On the playground Levien joins football matches with the children, retrieves errant footballs from the road with skilled kicks, and helps children climb to daring heights. I observed no such behaviour among the women staff, who preferred to stand around and talk to the children instead of actively playing with them.

Levien's image of his own masculinity came to the fore when I asked him how his teaching differs from that of women. His first response was his stated preference for sports and gymnastics over music and dance. Afterwards he explained his own use of outward signs of affection and the limits he imposes on himself, such as no kissing. He then continued by referring to himself as tough, using the word no less than five times in our conversation. He noted the benefits of this masculine trait for the development of both the boys and the girls in his class. He encourages them to be tough by encouraging them to refrain from complaining and by silently withstanding pain:

> In the beginning there was a lot of crying that children are having pain … from the wind or from somebody passing by or something, and that's over now. I think I make them tougher because I don't want them to come to me with every little pain, because when it's really painful I don't believe them if they are coming a hundred times before.

When a child gets pushed, Levien tells them: 'Be serious, don't whine.' If a child is having separation problems in the morning, he encourages them to overcome their sadness by sitting with him for a while. He actively models toughness for the children. He related to me an incident of having a thumbtack stuck in his finger and finding himself unable to remove it. He used this episode to teach the children about dealing stoically with pain:

> I was saying, 'Ok now, look, look, look', and I was smiling. And I said, 'It hurts, but I don't have to cry.' And I went to the other class to the first aid person and I told them, 'I can't get it out, could you help me?' And then after that I talked to the children and said, 'You see? It was painful but I didn't need to cry, it wasn't that bad. And then I told them a Dutch rhyme: Pijn is fijn, bloed is goed! (Pain is nice, blood is ok!).'

The Dutch refer to this phlegmatic display as 'nuchter', which means down to earth and practical. It has been considered by many to be a major trait of the

Dutch character. He situates his display of toughness in the context of caring. As he stated: 'I can be tough sometimes, but still when I'm tough I like [the children, and] I want them to be happy.'

As a man teaching young children, Levien prides himself in his support for rough-and-tumble play. 'With women it's different.' He recalled a comment made to him by a parent the previous year: 'I'm so glad you are here, my boy can be a boy.' Levien referred to this kind of play as 'a little struggle in a nice way'. He also noted that he keeps his eye on the situation so he can maintain acceptable boundaries of physical interaction: 'I know they can play a little bit physically and it goes well, so I allow them. I look at the kid and then I decide if I allow it or not, based on the fact that I know what they are capable of.' He tolerates rough-and-tumble play because he is in control and he sets the limits.

Levien's sense of his own masculinity finds expression in several aspects of his self-perception as well as in his unique teaching style. On the one hand, he tunes into the children's social and emotional needs, while on the other he shows a clear preference for their cognitive achievements. He outwardly shows signs of affection through touch, hugs and eye-level contact but these nurturing gestures are more like those of a caring father or a sweet female kindergarten teacher, which he rejects for himself. The two models are distinguished in his mind by the straightforward and instrumental discourse of the father compared to a more emotional and demonstrative approach of the archetypical female teacher of young children. He insists on clear boundaries for both his own playful attitude as well as his tolerance of boy play in the classroom. Levien works hard at achieving a careful balance between nurturing and toughness, as he maintains his position as a man who knows his work and deeply understands the needs of his young students.

The school and the society

While at the school I interviewed Eva van Oost, the school manager (principal), who had worked with Levien as a co-teacher before her promotion to her current position. She expressed a strongly positive attitude towards having men in the school, elaborating on the advantages of hiring them to work with children. She sees men as thinkers who reflect on their practice, while she characterizes women as doers. In terms of their work with children, she notices that men and women show gendered preferences for certain activities: men with sports and women with the sandbox and the jump rope. In her opinion children do not show partiality for men or women when they are in distress; however, the children do often choose one or the other according to the nature of the activity they prefer to engage in. She would like to achieve a balance in her school between men and women, to see more of a reflection of society at large. Consequently she engages in discriminatory hiring – preferring a man over a woman, considering that they are equally competent. Parents are generally in favour of having men teach young children, and only once during her two years as manager did she encounter opposition. In that case, the objection was so strong that the parents moved the child to a different school. In reflecting on why so few men choose the teaching profession, she notes the low salaries and lack of promotional career trajectories. However, she noted that in her experience, 'men always find a path of promotion out of the classroom', despite these limitations.

Along with the unstated hiring strategy that favours men, the school permits physical contact between teachers and students when appropriate, including young children sitting on their teachers' laps. This liberal policy stands in sharp contrast to a general fear in Dutch society of men as potential child abusers. During my five-day visit to the Netherlands, the newspapers were filled with stories about the sentencing of Robert M., a day care worker who had recently been convicted of 67 cases of child abuse, mostly children aged 3 months to 4 years, over a three-year period. At the time much public discourse centred on this traumatic case, which brought to the fore suspicions that men who work with young children are potential child abusers.

One response to such child abuse cases is the work of Lauk Woltring, an activist in promoting the inclusion of more men in the ECEC workforce as well as heightening public awareness of the specific educational needs of boys. To address the problem, he has published a ten-point programme in a paper entitled: 'Get the good guys in and the wrong guys out' (Woltring, 2012). In this article he recommends policies and strategies for identifying abusers, while encouraging men who are appropriate to enter the ECEC workforce. He claims that the overpublicized child abuse cases have damaged the image of men who choose to work with young children. In his words: 'This is a fact, so let's deal with it.' According to Woltring, the low level of men's participation in ECEC in the Netherlands (2–3 per cent) is a result of several factors: 'the public image of men, the tradition of women as caregivers, the female style and culture, and the professional educational work that is totally adjusted to female styles of working, communication, and raising children' (Woltring, 2009).

I took advantage of my brief visit to the Netherlands to meet Louis Tavecchio, Professor Emeritus of Research in Child Care at the University of Amsterdam. Professor Tavecchio is considered the country's leading expert on men in ECEC. As we enjoyed a cup of coffee on the banks of the Amstel River, our conversation encompassed many issues related to our mutual interest of understanding and increasing men's participation in the ECEC workforce. My colleague explained that there exists in the Netherlands a widespread belief that men doing women's work are likely to be gay. For example, male nurses are largely thought to be gay; and likewise men who work in ECEC. This assumption about sexual orientation coexists with open tolerance of homosexuals and lesbians. So while the public is not concerned about their child's kindergarten teacher being gay, they conflate homosexuality with child abuse, and are worried that the gay teacher may be a potential child molester. This phenomenon leads to a situation in which 'men are always defending themselves,' and these attitudes discourage men from entering the ECEC workforce.

Indeed, the percentage of men in elementary education is currently declining. While 15 per cent of elementary teachers are men, their number is expected to decrease to 10 per cent by 2020. Of the men who begin teacher training each year, 60 per cent drop out after six months because they find themselves in such a 'severe minority'. Agreeing with Woltring, Professor Tavecchio also claims that training institutions are to blame, as they are not geared to the needs of men. One such criticism has to do with men's antipathy towards endless reflection, which is one of the mainstays of the teacher training curriculum.

The Netherlands is a country that plans 25 years in advance for its public infrastructure and educational institutions. Therefore, it is no surprise that the former Dutch Secretary of Education, Halbe Zijlstra, has set a modest ten-year goal to increase the number of men in the elementary teaching force to 20 per cent, which contradicts Professor Tavecchio's prediction of a decrease. Children enter school at age 4 in the kindergarten, so men who are recruited for working in elementary schools may find their way into the kindergartens as well as the lower grades. One innovative attempt towards recruiting men is the project called 'Mannen Voor De Klas' ('Men in front of the class') (www.mannenvoordeklas.nu). In 2011, over 100 high school students in three cities were invited to local education colleges to learn about the possibilities of a teaching career. They were paired with men students at the college who worked with them to prepare lessons and activities for primary classes (ages 4–8). Wearing light blue hoodies with the project's logo, these young men went as a group to a primary school and taught their lessons under the tutelage of the local teachers. They then recounted their experiences, thereby generating a report with recommendations for increasing the number of men in the primary grades. A major emphasis in the report focused on the PABO (School of Education). Suggestions were made to recognize and address the needs of men who choose teaching as a career. The goal was to help these men, as a minority, achieve personal and professional satisfaction.

Levien and the system

Levien's story brings to the fore several issues about Dutch men as teachers of young children. The welcoming attitude of the Montessori network both pre-service and in-service provided an inviting venue for Levien. The leadership of the Montessori schools in the Netherlands nurtures a culture of openness and diversity, thus encouraging minority participation on many levels. Levien did his student teaching in the upper grades, but the job opening in kindergarten was offered to him. Considering the ambiguous climate in Dutch society surrounding men in ECEC, it took courage and vision on the part of the school leaders to place Levien with their youngest students.

From my perspective as an early childhood professional who knows how to recognize talent, I can say unequivocally that Levien landed in the right place. His fortuitous decision is a result of both personal and social factors. First of all, Levien knew himself well enough to reject his initial vocational choice of physiotherapy. Secondly, he exhibited openness to try an alternative suggested by friends. Like other societies, the Netherlands has many more men in primary teaching than in ECEC (15 per cent compared to 2–3 per cent). Thus the suggestion to consider primary teaching was gender feasible and not seen as totally bizarre. A third factor was the presence of another man in his class at the PABO. He claims that he would never have survived without such companionship and support, which corroborates Professor Tavecchio's assessment of the high dropout rate among men in pre-service teacher training.

Levien has found a comfortable place for himself as a man in his daily work. His focus on the cognitive aspects of learning fits with Montessori goals and his own temperament. Throughout the day, children play at learning tasks, which are duly recorded at their conclusion. While the children are stimulated cognitively by the task, Levien is stimulated cognitively by the challenges of the children's learning. Although throughout his teacher training he never expected to teach such young children, he has grown into the caring role that this job affords. As evidenced by his intense interest and concern for the children, he has found an acceptably masculine style of nurturing that includes touching within allowed boundaries and empathy towards the children.

Levien plans to move out of the kindergarten class as he progresses on a trajectory that he hopes will lead to a management position in the Montessori schools. His explanation for this plan is steeped in hegemonic masculine rhetoric: he needs to earn enough to support a family when he has one. At age 30, he feels that he has time to develop professionally and spend a few more years teaching, while keeping in mind his rational plan to achieve his ultimate career goal. His leaving the classroom for management will be a loss to Dutch society of a truly gifted early childhood educator.

Chapter 6

Eli Kruk

Kindergarten Teacher
Kfar Adumim, Judean Hills, Israel

'There's no learning without experience, and there's no experience without learning.'
Walking into Eli's kindergarten class feels like entering a petting zoo. The
first thing I observed during the morning free play time was the comfort and
ease with which the children dealt with the various small animals whose
cages were placed strategically around the room. A girl showed her friends
the corn snake wrapped loosely around her shoulders and a small group
of children played with the gerbils in their cage. Others hopped after the
rabbit, which they had placed on the floor after patting and lugging him
around. A toughened lizard clung to the shirt of another child, who showed
his friends his clever way of stimulating the sleepy reptile. Freed from its
cage, a parakeet jumped in staccato motion on nearby shelves, punctuating
the lively atmosphere with high-pitched monosyllabic shrieks. Two children
busied themselves cutting vegetables for the lizard's breakfast, while others
brought fresh water to the cages.

Eli was dressed for work, in casual cropped pants, a worn T-shirt and
sandals. Like many men in this small Judean desert community, he carried an
exposed pistol in a belt holder on his side. The children paid no attention to
the weapon, which was as much a part of their environment as the magnificent
desert surrounding their village. The kindergarten is located in Kfar Adumim,
a community where religious and secular Jews have chosen to live together,
about half an hour east of Jerusalem. Eli and his family of five live in the town
where he works.

Eli's presence was distinctly felt within this flurry of activity. At the
beginning of the day, he greeted each child and parent warmly, helping
the children choose an engaging activity with the animals or in one of the
many play venues such as the housekeeping area or the writing table. Each
of the 26 children was absorbed into the busy social milieu within minutes
of arrival. Throughout the morning, Eli involved the children in each stage
of the animals' care. Although his attention seemed to be instrumentally
focused on maintaining the cacophonous menagerie, he was concerned about
the needs of each child. For Eli, caring for these small animals is a means of
developing the children's responsibility and interacting with the children in

such a way as to honour their independence and nurture their emotional and intellectual growth.

Teaching young children was Eli's sole career choice. At the time of my observation, he was 35 years old, married with three children, and had been working in early childhood education for seven years. He told me that as a teenager, he knew that he wanted to do something of significance that would enable him to pass on values. His army service included three years of active duty and was integrated with two years of advanced Jewish studies in a yeshiva (an Orthodox Jewish institution of higher learning for religious studies). An officer himself, he trained others for a similar rank in combat duty. When his army service was drawing to a close, he thought about teaching in different contexts, and decided that formal instruction was not for him:

> I [considered] informal education or early childhood. I said that I will go for one of those two ... because here I know that I can influence as an educator, pave the way, put forth values and not just go into a classroom to say what I have to say and then leave, rather to give something, something beyond reciting facts. That's the reason that I went there.

He explained his decision to work with young children: 'My heart took me there.'

He was able to shorten his army service by a few months and chose to begin his studies immediately, instead of following the pattern of many young Israelis who at this transitional stage travel for extended periods in India or South America. Although religiously observant, he knew he would have to study early childhood education at a secular college because the religious institutions do not admit male candidates to the early childhood track. But even at the secular college he encountered 'raised eyebrows'. He had to convince the admissions committee that he would fit in, both in terms of 'gender' and his religious identity. In the end he was accepted into an honours programme that enabled him to complete the bachelor's degree and teaching licence in three instead of the usual four years with a full tuition scholarship. He majored in art within the early childhood track. The studies themselves were not difficult, and he found that his female colleagues 'indulged' him by bringing him class notes when he missed a lesson. As the only man in the programme of 100 women, he claims that the administration was often willing to 'round corners' for him, to make things a bit easier. Basically he had the same requirements as the women, with certain adaptations, such as working out in the fitness room while the women took swimming lessons.

Shortly after his graduation, he moved to the north of the country and was hired to teach 3-year-olds in a village preschool. After a year he relocated to a community near Jerusalem where he worked in a similar setting for two years. He then taught for two years in Jerusalem in a mixed-age special education setting. The next year he was hired in his current public school kindergarten job. Initially the facility belonged to the local Community Council but the Ministry of Education took responsibility for the kindergarten soon afterwards, which enabled Eli to benefit from the favourable working conditions offered by the Ministry. At the time of writing he had been employed in this job for five years. He worked and lived in the same community, and thus promoted a close relationship with the children's parents, who are his neighbours.

Eli's philosophy of education is based on respect for the child as an independent learner. For him, the kindergarten classroom must be a stimulating environment that arouses the child's curiosity and encourages exploration and discovery. As he said: 'There's no learning without experience, and there's no experience without learning.' He collaborates with the children to design the learning environment in such a way that they feel ownership, and this builds a sense of community among the children. However, he decides how the day will be organized and what the children will learn. At times he is willing to share this authority, but even then his leadership is strongly felt.

A day in Eli's class

My visit to the kindergarten took place on a hot summer's day in June, close to the end of the school year. The air-conditioned interior of the kindergarten contrasted sharply with the hot, dry environment of the desert surroundings. I managed to focus my scattered attention and turn from the various animals and their young caregivers to the charismatic orchestrator of this busy and productive learning microcosm. Eli's quiet energy was clearly the driving force behind the children's self-initiated learning. He regards the animals in the classroom as an opportunity to teach the living values of caring, responsibility, cooperation and independence. By setting up a habitat in which children and animals manage to live in delicate equilibrium, Eli patiently nurtures the children's natural curiosity and empathy for the animals. He has organized routines that enable the children to function with maximum independence while carrying out their responsibilities as caretakers for the various animals. Eli's double role of fostering independence while nurturing and caring was exemplified when he suggested that two boys prepare the lizard's morning salad. They brought chairs to the kitchen counter to stand on. Eli supplied them with blunt serrated knives, and demonstrated how to cut the carrot and cucumber into small enough pieces for the lizard to ingest. With the two children launched on their task, Eli moved on to mediating learning experiences with others. From time to time he returned to check up on the progress of the salad chefs. He wrapped his arms around them from behind, confirming the quality of their work and talking to them about the importance of this meal for the lizard. Having completed their task, the boys placed the salad in the cage, watching eagerly as the lizard gulped down the tiny bits of vegetable they had so fastidiously prepared.

As the day progressed, these themes of fostering independence within a framework of care and nurturing continued to crop up. At the morning meeting, children chose where to sit. The curriculum of the national religious school system includes a very brief morning prayer service, in which the children sang with lyrical passion, accompanied by an instrumental and voice recording. The content of the meeting was free ranging. Holding a Bible, Eli briefly mentioned episodes from the chapter they had been learning as he involved the children in the narrative highlights. Afterwards, he invited the children to plan activities for end-of-year party with parents, which was planned for the next day. Eli wanted the party to reflect the normal life of the kindergarten instead of a production that would require weeks of rehearsals. Characteristic of his participatory style of decision-making, he consulted them about which Bible story he would tell at the party and which songs the children would like to sing.

While they rehearsed their chosen songs, Eli gently brought a girl forward to stand in front of him, loosely holding her with both arms. He then moved around the circle, lightly tapping children on the head, signalling permission to move to the snack tables. Two others grabbed his legs and continued to hold on as he made his way around the circle. Having settled the group for their morning snack, he sat at a table with Reut, a girl who was eating alone. They enjoyed their light meal together, engaged in lively conversation. Once Reut had fully experienced this social engagement, Eli stood up and read a story to the entire group while they ate, stopping when he noticed a child crying, and dealing with the problem. He later explained to me that he likes to read a story during the meal to enable children to eat at their own pace. The slow eaters can finish their meal undisturbed while the faster ones can focus on the story until their friends finish. This series of events, from morning meeting to snack, shows Eli's passion for meeting the needs of the individual while maintaining the smooth functioning of the group.

Eli's leadership style includes setting limits for children and maintaining control over the programme, so effectively running the class. He feels that outdoor play time is important for all children, and everyone must play outside for the first half hour of the recess. 'Children who don't like [playing outdoors], don't like it because they're not good at it. And if they aren't good at it, they won't ever try it out.' At the beginning of the outdoor time, most of the children were quietly absorbed in activities related to sand and water play. Eli turned on a garden hose and upon request filled buckets and wheelbarrows with water which became the focus of play for the next hour. From time to time he playfully pointed the hose into the air, lightly sprinkling the children, much to their delight.

Having launched the sand and water play, Eli turned to a group interested in tending to the turtles. At the children's request, he removed turtles from their cage for children to play with on their own. He then selected a few children to help clean out the walk-in rabbit hutch. On their way to the rabbits, he hugged one of the boys from the side.

Once inside the huge cage, the children upended large sections of plastic pipe, and discovered newborn rabbits tumbling out. Eli asked his helpers emphatically not to touch the newborn rabbits so that their mother would continue to care for them, and he hastily ushered the children out of the cage. He explained to me later on that the newborn rabbits were dead, and he didn't want the children to see them. He added that he deals with loss and death of the animals, but in this case he thought it inappropriate for the children to be made aware of offspring that had been harmed by another animal. Eli turned the children's focus to the chicken coop, where they discovered and removed an egg laid by the hen that morning.

These events in the play yard demonstrate Eli's intense concern for providing appropriate play venues (sand and water); for encouraging the children's sense of responsibility (cleaning the rabbit hutch); and for monitoring their emotional well-being (turning their attention from a scene of possible mutilation to the pleasures of discovering a newly laid egg). Eli led these various episodes with a sense of nurturance as well as control, thereby achieving cooperation and joint purpose with the children.

Having propelled the children into their independent endeavours, Eli focused on his own projects. As he moved from one activity to the next, he involved interested children in each undertaking. While working on these ventures, Eli did not mediate in the children's play unless they called on him for assistance in executing a difficult task or in resolving interpersonal frictions. When his helpers collected insects from a beetle colony near the lizard's cage, Eli used tweezers to feed five of them one at a time to the hungry lizard while the children huddled around watching. This complex task required an adult but Eli managed to engage the children in a developmentally appropriate manner.

Eli again focused on his own project during the art activity time. He set out creative materials to be used freely at four tables. Instead of circulating among the tables and initiating conversation about the children's work, he set up his own project at another table in the middle of the room, collecting materials for large posters for three birthday celebrants. He composed the posters from small drawings made by the children at one of the art tables, gluing their pictures around a large photograph of the birthday child placed in the centre. Children hovered around him as he chatted with them while he worked. I was fascinated by the free movement of children: each child was expected to work at one of the art tables and then could move from table to table, or seek another play venue. This flowing movement exemplifies the independence of the children, who are all deeply engaged in their chosen activity just as Eli is. It occurred to me that by generating and executing his own artistic plans in full view of the children, Eli was modelling for them how to foster one's own sense of efficacy about creative work. His personal sense of fulfilment was clearly echoed in the children's pleasure in their self-initiated art work.

The play period at the end of the day was marked by two activities in which Eli clearly took the lead. For half an hour he sat at a table in the middle of the room and played a strategy card game, TAKI, with five children, while others watched from the side. He focused on teaching the children strategies to enhance their thinking and improve their chances of winning. He was frequently interrupted by children's questions or calls for help from other parts of the room. On occasion he raised his voice, asking rambunctious children to quieten down. After the game, Eli focused on preparing the room for the next day's family celebration to culminate the year by moving furniture to free up more space in the middle of the room and asking children to straighten up various play areas. Most cooperated as they accepted the shared goal of getting ready for the next day's event. Eli finished work at 2 p.m. when the afternoon staff arrived for the extended day programme. He said goodbye, giving children a light hug and brushing his hand through the hair of some of the girls. He and the children comfortably parted ways, as the children eagerly continued their programme with the afternoon staff.

I was astounded by the gender equality Eli managed to instil in the children throughout the morning. I could see no difference between the boys and girls in care of the animals, choice of play venues, or involvement in planning the end-of-year party. Boys prepared the lizard's salad with the same intensity that girls helped Eli move the furniture for the party. Not only were play gender roles indiscernible, but the interaction between the boys and girls showed no gender differentiation.

'My masculine essence'

Eli has well-articulated thoughts about the different contributions of men and women to early childhood education. He interpreted my question about this as a request to define the male personality but said he was not sure he could separate 'the male personality' from his own. However, he offered explanations of the unique contributions of men to the kindergarten based on his experience. According to Eli, men are more certain of themselves so they can demonstrate authority, achieving discipline more effectively than women. He suggested that such self-assurance might be a front to prove oneself a man but once it is achieved, it serves men well and discourages criticism. And a man's voice is more likely to project authority. Eli suggests that men have an entirely different approach to children and to dealing with their fear:

> When a child climbs on a tall chair a man and a woman will see this situation totally differently, regarding fears. For example, I work with pins. Someone will say, 'You'll get hurt.' So I say, 'So what?' So someone will get hurt, it will bleed, and we'll put on a plaster, or we'll kiss it, and we'll say: 'It's not so bad, so go ahead and [keep working]'.

Eli clearly believes that men encourage daring whereas women tend to be overprotective. He went on to explain gender differences in the kinds of activities men and women are likely to engage in. Men use tools, they build and they execute projects in the kindergarten that women would not undertake. Men have more time and energy to work on the physical environment of the classroom because they are not bound by the exigencies of running a household. He sees himself as an extremely social and outgoing person, and this bolsters his camaraderie with the fathers of the children in his class. He particularly enjoys Friday mornings because of the chance to chat with them in a relaxed manner. Most men in his community have the day off in preparation for the Sabbath and they (instead of their wives) bring their children to kindergarten. Eli misses this male dialogue on other days.

Eli believes that men have advantages and limitations when working with children. He sets limits for himself on touching and intimacy by avoiding situations where he might find himself alone with a child, especially in the toilets. Although he has no problem wiping bottoms, he makes sure that another adult is present. Throughout the day, he holds children, swings them around, and allows them to hang on to his legs but he will not sit a child in his lap lest this be misconstrued as excess intimacy. For Eli, men have their own lexicon of movement, and he actually warns himself against imitating the movements of women:

> If you imitate the movement of women, people will think you are a homo. You won't be you, the male kindergarten teacher, and you won't be [an authentic] female teacher either. But the moment you are a male teacher, accept it. You are a male teacher with the drum, you sing with the children, and you dance with them, and you do it with less delicate movements, because men are built differently. You look different, and you move differently.

For Eli gender differences go beyond interaction with the children; they flow into the realms of motivation and career. He claims that women often choose early childhood teaching out of convenience while men choose it out of commitment to ideals, which indicates greater passion in working with the children. Men are interested in career advancement while women tend to be satisfied with remaining in the same job until retirement. Gender roles in Eli's kindergarten are divided very traditionally. His female aide cleans and washes the room and decorates the walls. Eli builds, creates and initiates. He carries a pistol in his belt: 'I would rather have [the gun] if I need it than be unarmed and be unable to protect the children if something [a terrorist act] were to happen.' However, he feels that gender balance in the kindergarten is essential so there are male and female role models for all the children, who may at times need one role model or the other. Eli summarized his feelings about himself as a man in the kindergarten: 'I bring my entire masculine essence to this job.'

Support from close up and afar

Eli's success as a kindergarten teacher is certainly due largely to his personal charisma and his professional skills. In addition, he has located himself in a supportive community that is open to change and new ideas. The community of Kfar Adumim, with a current population of 2,500, was founded in 1979 on the ideology of secular and religious Jews living together in harmony. This is rare in the religious communal culture, which is largely composed of idealistic national religious Jews who tend to isolate themselves physically from the secular world, thus enabling a lifestyle that emphasizes religious practice. While most of the public schools in the country divide along sectorial lines, the kindergartens and elementary school in Kfar Adumim purposefully integrate the two cultures both socially and programmatically. This openness to differences paved the way for hiring a man in the community's kindergarten. Eli senses parental approval and support of his position as one of the community's early childhood educators. I was impressed by his puzzled reaction to my question about possible suspicion among parents. He told me that in the beginning, having a man teacher was a 'gimmick', a positive move to wave a liberal flag, because 'this is something that isn't yet accepted'. As a veteran teacher of ten years, he claims that he has moved beyond the stage of parental concerns about possible paedophilia. Eli feels that after parents got to know him 'face to face' and saw 'who I am', any apprehensions evaporated. He currently enjoys wall-to-wall parental approval and for years has not encountered any misgivings. Beyond some initial issues with parents, Eli faced difficulties at first with the woman who worked as his aide. When she realized that she had to do the same work in the kindergarten with a man as with a woman, she calmed down and accepted him. At the time of this interview, Eli's relationship with this aide was characterized by mutual respect and assistance: 'We aren't teacher and aide, we are partners, totally.'

To gain a broader perspective on the cultural and administrative context in which Eli works, I interviewed Ziona ben Hemo, the inspector from the Ministry of Education for the region and Eli's direct supervisor. In more than two decades on the job, Ziona has had largely positive experiences in hiring three men on her teaching staff at different times:

> My relatively broad experience with men in the position of preschool teacher testifies to my openness and understanding that men can also work in early childhood. I truly think that this is not women's work alone. I do not 'screen out' candidates because of their gender.

Although she hired one young man in the past as fill-in staff whose work was terminated after two years because 'he didn't invest himself in the work', she hired a second man, who proved excellent. He quit after some time in order to establish his own private nurseries, a not uncommon move by the Israeli men who enter the profession (Perez, 2009).

Ziona does not use preferential hiring practices for men. She claimed that Eli went through the same selection process as the women. Once she hired him she was impressed by the community's sincere acceptance of a man in the job. 'There were no raised eyebrows.' She attributes the parents' approval of Eli to the general openness that characterizes the Kfar Adumim community, which has, she says, publicly 'proclaimed their ethos of acceptance and inclusion. This is a community which cannot say "no" to a man as a kindergarten teacher. Eli's acceptance as a kindergarten teacher was one more proof of their openness.'

She contrasted Eli's acceptance to the situation with the second man she hired in a different community characterized by its middle-class upward mobility. There she found parents who had some reservations but made no protest. She managed to convince them to give the teacher a chance and to watch him in action. The strategy paid off when the teacher proved his abilities in the classroom and earned broad parental acceptance. But an unexpected problem arose when the female aide refused to work with a man and her husband requested that his wife be transferred to a classroom with a woman teacher. After discussions with the teacher himself, the aide's husband agreed that she would remain in the classroom with him and they worked together successfully.

I asked Ziona for her views about differences between men and women in the role of early childhood teacher. Her first comment related to the constraints of an employee who is obligated to active army reserve duty. With universal conscription in Israel, many men continue to serve in reserve units until their forties and are called up for reserve duty for a few days up to two or three weeks a year. State inspectors have to find substitutes, often on the spur of the moment.

Ziona sees gender differences related to the way men and women function in the classroom. Men have little sense of classroom aesthetics: 'They care less about enhancing the physical learning environment than about interacting with the children.' This requires attention because she values 'aesthetic education' as an integral part of the young child's overall education. She tries to respect Eli's judgement regarding the physical atmosphere of his class but claims that Eli has chosen to assign responsibility for classroom aesthetics to his (female) aide. He has come to accept this division of labour, although he believes in his own artistic preferences, which differ from his supervisor's. Ziona notes Eli's effectiveness in both the speed and the breadth of his written planning, which equal those of her best female teachers. Ziona sees a difference in dealing with children's interpersonal conflicts: whereas women tend to ponder the situation and see shades of grey, men make quick decisions because they see reality more in black-and-white terms.

When asked about a man teacher's physical contact with the children, Ziona reminded me that men candidates are screened by the Ministry of Education, and must bring police evidence that they have no record of criminal offence. She is comfortable with normal physical contact between her men teachers and the children: 'I place no limitations. I think it is wrong to place limitations. I believe that children deserve and need warmth and love and physical contact. It doesn't matter who the significant adult is who works with the child.' With 145 teachers under her supervision, Ziona's visits to Eli's class are relatively more frequent than to other kindergarten classes. Eli senses her complete backing, and this gives him licence to function as he sees fit in his own isolated and supportive community.

Masculinity in Israeli society

Conventional male hegemony has played a major role in Israeli culture. The early Zionists who founded the state rejected the traditional image of diaspora diaspora Jewish men who focused their energies on passively studying the holy books. In the first half of the 20th century, they replaced this view with the masculine model of the manual worker, the initiator and the defender, thus establishing a masculine ideal as a core value of the society they were building. Women were given important roles which included agricultural field work, manual building and some minor defence roles. Both male and female gender roles were under scrutiny and reconstruction. The early kibbutzim organized themselves in such a way that mothers were freed from caring for their own children so they could take on other work roles.

The incessant security threat from the neighbouring Arab states since the country's establishment in 1948 has given the army a central role as the nation's major socializing agent. Even children are involved in this warrior narrative from a young age (Furman, 1999). All Jewish men and women are subject to conscription with exemptions for religious women and almost the entire ultra-Orthodox male population. Connell (2005) has described the military as the main agent in inculcating social gender roles. In Israel, the almost universal engagement of men both in active duty and then as reserves until their mid-forties reinforces the national ethos of men as protectors and women as protected (Klein, 1999). This gender division is reinforced in the army, where women soldiers are typically assigned socially oriented and clerical tasks, providing a softer side to the male atmosphere. It was only in 2000 that women were allowed to take on combat duties in the army. For men, service in the Israeli army has been thought to function 'as a rite of passage to male adulthood' (Klein, 2002: 671), giving the soldiers an opportunity to prove themselves as men. Another important aspect of army masculinity is the nurturance of camaraderie among the soldiers. Deep personal relationships are typically built in the army units, which function socially as well as strategically, and these significant friendships often last well into the future beyond the day of discharge (Kaplan, 2006).

For young men from the national religious sector of society, this traditional Israeli masculine ethos is tempered by a different gender paradigm.

Many of these men elect to spend one to five years in a yeshiva, where they integrate advanced Judaic studies with their army service. This period serves as a transition from high school into the army and into later civilian life as well. The image of the yeshiva student is one of 'erudition and refinement' (Sheleg, 2013), feminine traits that sharply contrast with the masculine supremacy cultivated in the army. The military experience emphasizes 'physical strength … emotional control, and managing under conditions of pressure and stress' (Amar Levy, 2013). Sheleg (2013) claims that these opposing dispositions create among these young men a duality that they continue to deal with as they are discharged from the army, complete their yeshiva studies and enter civilian life. Family is a central value and they marry young and have several children by their early thirties. They are challenged by the need to carve out a fathering role as they engage in the care of their young children (Huri, 2013). Their gender-segregated religious high schools ill prepare them for this task. There, the boys are acculturated to believe that women should hold very conventional female roles in the family, although both daughters and sons are expected to help with household chores and care for the younger brothers and sisters.

The young men's partners are wives who are studying and/or working (Alkobi, 2008), and the men tend to involve themselves routinely with the care of their children. Thus the duality described by Sheleg supports a softening of their military masculinity, and allows them to move into a different place that nurtures the more traditionally feminine traits they learned in yeshiva. This morphing of the militaristic masculinity among young men in the national religious camp is reflected in contemporary Israeli cinema (Rivlin, 2013). A recent review of current Israeli films and television serials reveals how Israeli men have discovered the failure of traditional masculinity both in modern combat as well as in civilian life. Rivlin suggests that in these films both secular and religious men look back to gender norms learned in the army, and 'come to realize that they have already missed the boat of tough manliness' (Rivlin, 2013: 44). This dissonance leads to a re-examination of these traditional values, and to the possibility of a softer and more considered model of manliness.

In his teaching, Eli exemplifies both sides of Israeli masculinity: the traditional militaristic ethos alongside the image of the caring father. In both the interviews with Eli, he failed to mention his service in the IDF (Israel Defence Force) except to tell me about his decision to study education afterwards. Omissions in personal narratives can reveal ambivalence about segments of one's past (Tuval and Spector-Marzel, 2010). Having lived in Israel for 25 years, I am acutely aware of the importance of army service for men of any age so I decided to question him about his military service in a subsequent conversation. Only then did he inform me that he had served as an officer in a combat unit and had trained other officer candidates.

Once I heard the full story, I could fit the pieces of Eli's narrative together. Eli sees his guardian role as an inherent aspect of his unquestioned masculinity, both in his kindergarten job and as a responsible male citizen in a threatened society – hence the pistol. His views about role divisions in the kindergarten also fitted this image of masculine hegemony. His female aide is assigned the cleaning tasks as part of her official job description, and prefers to focus on the physical needs of the children and the aesthetic appearance of the classroom. Eli, meanwhile, supervises the children in their care of the animals, builds outdoor cages for the menagerie, and initiates the educational programme. When furniture needs to be moved for the end-of-year performance, it is Eli who takes charge. Ziona has noted these gendered differences in his mode of leadership and suggested that this style is modelled on the military commander. For example, Eli playfully uses the Hebrew command 'kadima', which means 'forward', when he wants the children to get up and move out, which Ziona calls 'a little bit masculine'.

It is no wonder that Eli expresses his masculinity in such visible terms, considering the exaggerated gender role divisions in Israeli society. Maintaining his male identity is critical to his successful functioning. In 2011, fewer than 15 men enrolled in ECEC programmes out of a student population of 400–500 (Tzaban, 2012). More significantly, men compose less than 0.1 per cent of the early childhood workforce (CBS, 2004). So few men studying ECEC and teaching young children creates an extreme sense of 'otherness' among the few men who do choose this career (Sumision, 2000).

Perez (2009) identified three aspects of this 'otherness' identity. The first is related to a Hebrew linguistic norm requiring use of the male verb, noun and adjective forms when addressing the public, even if only one member of the audience is a man. In the past when no men were present, women at gatherings of early childhood educators were accustomed to being addressed with female linguistic forms. With a man in the group, the language of the entire meeting shifts to the masculine form. This linguistic feature of male hegemony emphasizes the presence of the singular man among a room full of women colleagues, and causes him considerable discomfort. A second aspect of otherness emerges in the first days of school when parents are surprised to find a man in the role of kindergarten teacher. These teachers have often been mistaken as the father of a child because of the almost unimaginable possibility that the role might be filled by a man.

The third is the contrast between the man's relative ease at entering the ECEC job market and the negative reactions he hears from parents when he first begins work. This ambivalence grows out of preferential positive hiring treatment and college field placements on the one hand, and parents' suspicions about homosexuality and paedophilia on the other. Thus the ever-present feeling of being different provides an ongoing challenge for Israeli men who have chosen to work with young children and have stepped out of the gender boundaries that were so clearly defined in their army service. In response to this feeling of otherness, they typically draw succour from their military male identity.

Against this backdrop of classic masculinity that Eli displays in various ways, I found a softer, caring side in his fatherly manner with the children and in his nurturance of the small animals in his classroom. Hugs and other forms of physical contact are de rigueur. His decision to eat lunch with Reut, the little girl who did not find her social niche at the snack table, is one small but significant indicator of Eli's nurturance. The duality of masculinities described by Sheleg (2013) explains Eli's style and the complexity of his interactions with the children. He is their protector, but he also empowers both the girls and the boys to function as a microcosm of an egalitarian society. He divides adult tasks in the kindergarten along traditional gender lines, but he expects the children to function equally in carrying out their responsibilities in the classroom.

By choosing early childhood as his field of endeavour, Eli has challenged the traditional social gender roles of his community. And he has taken the more feminine aspects of yeshiva learning, erudition and refinement, and turned them into an alternative and respectable model for Israeli men in his national religious subculture. Fathers enjoy chatting with him on Friday mornings when they drop off their children. For them, Eli is not the other, but one of the tribe. As a respected member of both his professional and social community, Eli has turned the 'otherness' of a man teaching young children into a possible lifestyle. His modelling fits with the changing role of men in Israeli society, and places him in a leadership position as an innovator and initiator of social change.

Leon Mahon

Chapter 7

Leon Mahon

Nursery Caregiver, Mary Sambrook Day Nursery
London Borough of Tower Hamlets, East London, UK

'Entering the world of the child'

A young mother hands her whimpering daughter, Soma, to Leon and hurries out of the nursery room to get to work on time, leaving her behind. Leon scoops up the 18-month-old in his arms, speaking soothingly as he shows her the large colourful Duplo displayed on a nearby table. When Soma begins to show interest in the toy, Leon sets her gently on a chair and they work together to stack the blocks into a jagged tower. Leon's 12 years of experience with toddlers at an East London nursery have prepared him well for this stressful scenario. His quiet assurance gently broadcasts that everything is going to work out fine no matter what the challenge. Such scenes are not unusual, as the families served by the nursery are often under stress. According to Hana Kovler, the manager of the successful Mary Sambrook Day Nursery, the London Borough of Tower Hamlets in East London has a large Muslim population (42 per cent), of mainly Bangladeshi origin. The borough itself is reported to have the largest percentage of child poverty in the UK – 48.6 per cent in 2010 (Ryan, 2013). Julian Grenier, Early Years Advisor to Tower Hamlets at the time of my visit, explained that many children in the nursery have been referred by social workers due to issues of concern about poor thriving, health needs or learning disabilities. Only a very few are enrolled at full tuition for a full-time placement.

Leon was born and grew up in East London, in a family of Irish immigrants. His mother worked in an office and his father rose through the ranks in a stock brokerage firm and eventually opened his own brokerage business. Although he did not speak at great length about his childhood and adolescence, Leon's school experience had clearly been adverse. He left school just before his 16th birthday after completing O-level exams. He was unemployed for extended periods of time, floating from job to job. As he eloquently described his situation: 'I had long periods of studying and metaphysical drifting and unemployment. I was interested in doing writing for very small independent magazines.' During this time he began playing bass guitar in a rock band called The Assassins of Hope. 'We don't really make any money. We produce our own CDs. Yeah, I still enjoy it, after all these years.' It wasn't until he reached age 24 that he decided to complete his A-levels in Communications and English Language and Literature in an adult education setting. Two years later, he found himself floating between various college courses, 'some I dropped out [of] and some I continued.' With no particular focus in life but with an eye on finding a job, he listened to his friends and family, who told him that they liked the way he interacted with nieces and nephews and with friends' children and asked: 'Have you ever thought of working with children? You seem to have a really good connection with them.'

His long-time girlfriend showed him a newspaper advert for a training programme through the Preschool Learning Alliance for playgroup work. He agreed to try it out, enrolled, and completed the course by studying and doing a work placement two days a week over a two-year period. He was not enthusiastic about the prospect of working in a nursery, which he considered another 'dead end', so he enrolled in a second course for the job of learning support assistant. These teachers work in schools or preschools with children needing special attention. While on the course, he saw a newspaper announcement for a nursery job with infants and toddlers. 'I thought that I would go [to the interview] almost for interview practice ... I got the job. That's it.' This was a turning point in his life. He has remained at the Mary Sambrook Day Nursery for 12 years working with a mixed age and ability group of infants and toddlers. Early on he took the National Vocational Qualifications (NVQ) Level 3 course, studying on day release for two years. This earned him the title of childcare worker, a rise in salary and job security.

Although his father had hoped that Leon would choose to go into his brokerage business, in the end he supported Leon's career decision, although with a few 'question marks related to it being a job more associated with females ... My dad has been very supportive in whatever I have chosen to do in my life ... He just wanted [me and my siblings] to find happiness in whatever we chose to do'. His mother was happy to see him 'settling down'. As Leon said bluntly, 'at least it was a job'. His friends were generally positive, though some thought it 'an odd choice of career'. He described these friends as not 'stereotypically macho men', and with them he became involved in the anarchist punk music scene of the early 1980s 'that valued ideas above musical proficiency'. Although his decision to teach in the nursery 'was a bit unusual, coming out of the blue', most of his friends were supportive and 'quite interested in how I was doing'.

His experience on the A-level course strengthened his resilience as a loner in the group. As 'a lone mature student' and one of the few non-Bangladeshi trainees in the childcare preparation class, he managed to get along well with the younger Bangladeshi students. Both the teacher and Leon's female classmates were fairly positive towards him. As a man he was not expected to exhibit a natural talent for childcare so his positive performance earned him high regard. Leon reported the reaction of the women in the class when he showed that he could work well with babies: 'Wow, he's a man and he can do that!' He said that: 'It was like I get a shiny star.' His focused work orientation laid the foundation for his positive feelings about the course which he found to be a useful preparation for the job of nursery childcare worker.

A description of his work in the nursery adds depth to Leon's story of how he became a nursery childcare worker and why at age 40 he has continued in the job. The way he interacts with the children illustrates the positive outcomes of his earlier career decisions.

A day in Leon's toddler group

My visit to the nursery was not well timed. At the end of the summer the enrolment was in flux, because the older 3-year-olds had moved on to preschool settings, and younger children had not yet begun. Like all the rooms at the nursery, the Star room has children aged from 18 months to 3 years, and usually contains 11 children with three staff. But on this day only four children appeared at drop-off time and two more came in later. With two childcare workers and a learning support assistant for these few children, I was doubtful I would see Leon in action. As my observation began I soon realized that I had completely underestimated Leon's expertise as a caregiver for this young age, as well as his quiet charisma. For a start, he was tuned in to the emotions of very young children. This being the second day for several of them, separation from the parent was still traumatic. Among the staff present on that day, it was Leon who initiated picking up each crying child, comforting them, and enticing them into playing. A gentle touch and a simple conversation focused on the child's play eased their painful transition from home.

Leon's heightened sensitivity to the children came to the fore in the play yard when he once again found himself surrounded by children despite the presence of three other caregivers. This time, the children were well launched into their activities for the day. They had climbed onto a small platform inside a plastic climber that featured a slide. Leon squirmed into this small structure, standing next to and behind two children who were busily engaged in bouncing up and down, enjoying the give and take of the plastic floor on which they were standing. For several minutes, Leon resonated with their movements, speaking to them, enjoying the delight of a 2-year-old's discovery that when you bounce, the whole assembly shakes. Not once did Leon claim an adult agenda that might have included encouraging them to go down the slide. He was totally in synch with them, and his empathy expressed physically through his body language and speech as he talked to them about bouncing. When a third child approached, Leon gently lifted her onto the platform so that she too could join in the parallel play. Only when the children tired of bouncing, did Leon suggest using the slide. Once again, his timing was perfect. Now he managed each child individually, dealing with their bravado or their fears as they met the challenge of coming down from the platform.

Leon's uncommon ability to connect and extend the children's thinking was again obvious at the outdoor water table. Two children were busily pouring from one vessel to another. He squatted to their eye level and talked to them about their efforts, respecting their decisions to pour clumsily from wide to narrow vessels. He met their less successful attempts with smiling approval and suggested alternative containers. At one point he tried his own experiments, setting up a system of pouring water from a smaller to a larger container, and acting as though this was the most amazing and interesting discovery anyone could possibly have made. His quiet manner and endless patience were coupled with enlightened sensitivity to the inner world of the children. Although these qualities appear to be intuitive, Leon uses them with sincere intention.

I noted how Leon encouraged the children's independence. Young children desire independence naturally. Leon capitalized on this by sharing responsibilities and showing them how a particular activity could be carried out. For example, instead of putting a plastic apron on each child as they came to the water table, he sent her to a large basket to select an apron and bring it back to him. Then he helped her put on the apron before playing with the water. I also noted how he taught behaviour that he wanted the children to integrate into their own repertoire. At lunch, he not only asked each child which food they wished to eat but also encouraged them to dish out their own portion. He respected their wishes without applying pressure and without suggesting what they should be choosing to eat. At the end of the meal, he led each child to the food trolley and showed them how to scrape the remains from their plate into a scrap bowl and how to put their cutlery into a bowl of water. As they scraped, he counted to ten. Such actions would have been more easily performed by the adult, but Leon has independence high on his learning agenda, so he takes the time and effort to teach them to perform these simple tasks by themselves. Leon said that all staff at the nursery are encouraged to enable children to be independent and to be supportive and caring and he has clearly internalized these values, incorporating them into his daily practice.

Care is an inseparable part of Leon's relationship with the children. He demonstrated this primarily through his sensitive attitude towards the needs of the children and by his follow-through with verbal and physical actions. I have noted how he calmly lifted Soma when she showed distress and spoke to her not about her sadness, but about building with Duplo. With almost no outward display of emotion, no kisses or exaggerated hugs, Leon's action communicated to the child a powerful message: 'I'm in control, I like you, you are safe with me, and I'm going to help you find something interesting to do right now.' When a child's nappy needed to be changed, Leon calmly carried her to the toilets, talking and singing as he performed the task. He emerged from the toilets with the child either in his arms or following behind him. He then transitioned the child into the next activity with calm assurance.

Leon also demonstrated his unique brand of caring when helping the toddlers relax into their afternoon nap. He set up the room so each child has a large round pillow, a sheet and a blanket, then offered them a selection of soft toys. If the child wanted to lie down on their own, he helped them into a comfortable position, covered them and rubbed their back for a bit. With the more reluctant sleepers, he sat on the floor next to the pillow, extending his legs comfortably, and offered the child the possibility of leaning against him as he gently patted their back. If this strategy did not work and the child walked over to the classroom door, Leon determined that she did not need a nap and should be delivered to the hands of nursery caregiver on the other side of the door to play with others who had chosen not to nap. These three incidents illustrate different examples of Leon's caring, which is characterized more by practical actions that meet the child's needs than by displays of emotion.

My understanding of Leon's day-to-day functioning was enriched in an interview with Lorraine Khelfi, the nursery's deputy manager. She summarized Leon's unique style of caregiving thus: 'He is particularly good at talking to children, talking things through. He talks in a calm way.' She noted his initiatives, such as bringing his guitar for the children to strum and explore. She stressed his love of physical activities and his enrolment on a brief training course to lead physical education activities at the nursery in a programme called 'Top Start'. Lorraine believes that Leon serves as an important male role model for children whose fathers are absent or who have little involvement in their children's upbringing. One girl bonded strongly with Leon at 17 months, and now at age 3 she is 'level headed and well developed', an accomplishment that Lorraine lays at the feet of Leon's early care and attention.

Professional identity

Although my morning observations provided an insightful view of Leon's style of working with children, the experience left me extremely curious about how he views himself as a nursery childcare worker. At the end of the long working day, when all the children had been picked up, I was rewarded with a lengthy, relaxed and open interview with him in the parent lounge at the nursery. Leon freely shared his own narrative about how he came to this current job and his reflections about his work, work relations, and his views on children and childcare.

Leon is filled with wonder at the world of childhood, which he calls 'a magical time'. He expressed his enthusiasm for entering the children's magical world through imaginative play: 'They'll be playing roles of monsters and they'll say, "Leon can you be the monster?" and they will run and hide, and I will creep around and kind of half scare them, just that nice sort of scariness, where they really love it.'

He especially enjoys physical activity with the children, which he sees as being particularly male. This includes playing outdoors in various kinds of gross motor actions: 'I spend a lot of time throwing balls or kicking, yeah, so I also like a lot of bouncing and climbing, and things like that. They seem to enjoy doing that and I obviously enjoy [it] … and that's why the children see me as the person to do that.'

Leon will also spontaneously act silly, and this brings pleasure to him and the children, such as impersonating an elephant who eats sticky buns. These three styles of engaging children – imaginary play, physical activity and silliness – form the core of Leon's delight in his work and fulfil his desire to in some way become a child again: 'It kind of takes you back into your own childhood.' He pointed out that some of his female colleagues share his approach to children while others 'fulfil a more motherly role'.

Leon believes in the importance of forging a 'really strong connection with the child'. This goal has several components, the most essential being his desire 'to enter into their world'. By this he means looking closely and 'seeing what interests them or what motivates them or just how they enjoy themselves'. He wants to be 'accepted by them' so that 'you feel relaxed with them and they feel relaxed with you'. In addition to being comfortable with him, he also wants them to be comfortable with the environment and with themselves.

These well-articulated goals are the product of 12 years of committed work with toddlers. Leon has grown into the job. Although he at first viewed his employment at the nursery as little more than a relatively well-paid form of stable work, he has developed very positive feelings about his contribution to the current well-being and the future of the children: 'I mean, if I look at my life in terms of my whole life, I do realize the value of what I do.' He is happy with his current role, but has considered working with older children. He sees his place as caring for the children and has no intentions of moving into management. I was interested in his future plans so I asked him to visualize where he might be ten years hence. He found this a difficult question to answer. It seems that his inertia in remaining in the toddler room is tinted with ambivalence. This may stem from dissonance between his thoughts about himself as a middle-aged man and the enjoyable reality of daily work with the toddlers. He reflected on my question: 'I haven't really [pause] planned for where I'm going from here … I can't imagine working here in ten years' time, put it that way.'

Masculinity in East London

As the only man childcare worker at the Mary Sambrook Day Nursery, Leon must constantly define his masculinity within the context of his co-workers and his friends. When he first began working at the nursery he was not accepted by all his colleagues: two women 'didn't make me feel very welcome, and I couldn't decide if it was because I was kind of a bit shy and a male coming into a different world and wasn't sure of myself.' He later decided that their dissatisfaction with their own jobs led to a form of scapegoating at his expense. The mild hostility that he experienced from them was balanced by support from 'the majority'. Despite this general acceptance, his initiation into the female realm of caregiving was problematic for two reasons: his gender and his lack of experience in caring for infants and toddlers. He was viewed by some of the other caregivers as an outsider on both counts. From his own experience, Leon distinguished between the mother and father roles by suggesting that the matriarch is strict and toes the line, while the father figure is indulgent, a role that is more comfortable for him than that of the disciplinarian. He finds setting limits difficult, although he has tightened up in this realm over the years. He referred to this duality of mother and father figures and the veteran women on the staff:

> I found that I wasn't able obviously to do that matriarchal role and
> sometimes I didn't feel as strong as they were and they were able
> to do the [pause], being strict, if you want to call it that, when they

needed to be, with a child, and I didn't feel as strong as they were,
to be quite honest and that made me feel ... I was being judged.

Over time he has become used to being in a minority of one, although another
man at the nursery works as a learning support assistant. He claims that he
likes being in an extreme minority, and that he 'gets on very well with co-
workers now'. He copes with this reality by defining a man's niche in this
women's world. Leon sees himself as a gentle person, and suggests that both
men and women can appreciate 'the gentler side of the male personality'. He
found such recognition and appreciation from his former long-term girlfriend,
who wholeheartedly supported his decision to work in the nursery. While
many women do the job of caregiver naturally because they are mothers, he
has had to work hard at learning the role.

In defining his masculine self vis-à-vis the women's typology, he notes
several aspects of his behaviour which differ from that of the women with
whom he works. He prefers physical over sedentary activity with the children,
he likes fantasy and superhero games, and he enjoys being silly. He defines all
three as particular to men. He claims that children initiate physical contact
with him, such as grabbing him around his leg, which they do not do to the
women. This type of physical connection, which he views as particular to
himself as a man, seems to result from the rough-and-tumble play that he
initiates and enjoys. The deputy manager, Lorraine, confirmed this aspect of
men's work with young children, describing other men with whom she has
worked in the past: '... rough and tumble on the carpet, let kids jump all over
him. [Another man caregiver was] older, a bit more refined. Got to their level.
He was excellent with children with challenging behaviour and showed a
world of patience.'

Leon believes that the staff now recognize his unique masculine
contribution. Firstly, he fills the father role for children from single-parent
families, of which there are many. Secondly, he provides a male role model that
is nurturing and diverges from what the children see elsewhere. Leon claimed
that his presence benefits the children by offering an alternative gender role,
thus enriching the children's early years' experience. Because of his interest
in sports, he was training in the 'Top Start' physical education programme.
His beneficial influence is also recognized by parents, especially at the end of
the year, when many told him that they see him as a 'positive person in their
child's life'. He summarized his thoughts about this affirmative assessment:
'I've been very happily surprised by it because of the positive response of 99
per cent of the parents I've worked with.'

Leon's successful coping with these gender issues sits in the foreground of underlying stress caused by society's negative view of men in the caregiving role. Over the years, he has encountered five or six incidences of parents not wanting him to change their child's nappies. These cases were resolved by having a female co-worker take this on. The staff team have been advised to exercise caution in how they position themselves, for example, when they change a child's nappy, so their actions cannot be misconstrued. However, every time the mass media in Britain reports on a child abuse case, even among women childcare workers, Leon feels the anti-male bias rears its ugly head. Although all potential workers must obtain police clearance exonerating them from any criminal record, Leon feels that he is sometimes under suspicion for no reason other than his gender. 'So these are the kind of issues that come up specifically about being a male childcare worker. As a male I have to be partly aware all the time that my interactions with the children cannot be misconstrued, but to be over-concerned would make proper interaction impossible.'

These stressful incidents have on occasion caused Leon to reconsider his occupational choice. 'It would be so traumatic that I sometimes think that this isn't the sort of job for me. I have thought that sometimes, very occasionally, yeah.'

Leon notes other issues that also mitigate against men's success in childcare work. Extreme gender isolation is one of the most weighted concerns. Not only is he the sole male caregiver at the Mary Sambrook Day Nursery but he has never in his 12 years on the job met another man in the same role. He claims that there are no other men in attendance at professional development meetings, except an occasional primary teacher working in the lower grades. Hana Kovler, the nursery manager, confirmed this when she told me that there is only one other male worker in the entire borough whom Leon might well have never met. I was astounded to hear Leon's comment in our interview. For a moment I found myself stepping outside my skin as an objective researcher and sympathizing with Leon and his situation. Having experienced this kind of isolation myself as a childcare worker, I was moved when he told me he would like to know how many men actually work as caregivers in England and 'would be interested to meet other men who work in this [field].' Leon appeared unable to view himself as one among men in the nursery he could identify with and draw support from. Leon sees the dearth of men in the nurseries as a major hindrance to attracting more men into the field, yet despite being the only man on the staff, Leon feels valued at the nursery. His feelings echoed mine when I was the only man in a day care centre and was esteemed by my supervisors and peers.

Leon has encountered an additional difficulty, namely presenting himself and his work to other men. He enjoys football matches and sometimes finds himself in a problematic situation after the game:

> Let's say you're at the bar having a drink and someone says, 'Oh what's your job, mate?' – kind of like that. Now I'd probably think this is a bit dodgy, you know … But I'd normally say 'I just work with young children', and they would say 'in what kind of school?' and I would say 'in a nursery'. Sometimes people would look at you kind of funny, a bit dodgy, make a joke around me, that type of thing … You still have to explain yourself a little bit more. You know people.

My American lexicon did not prepare me for the word 'dodgy'. I pursued its meaning enthusiastically because I felt it was a key to understanding Leon's message. What Leon means is to be under suspicion or driven by questionable motives, so he is concerned lest his pub mates think he has chosen this line of work because of either a criminal interest in child molestation or a gay sexual orientation. As a heterosexual with a female partner, Leon is able to cope with these occasional suspicions by arming himself with a positive self-image about his work with young children. 'I mean I don't care whether people think I'm gay, straight, or bisexual. Yeah, I really don't. Yeah I'm quite happy with [my work], so it doesn't worry me.' Leon holds no prejudices against people who choose a gay lifestyle, and is more likely to take offence at being suspected of child abuse than at aspersions about his sexual orientation. His positive work identity seems like a defence that he wears in the face of peer acceptance issues, the threat of child abuse accusations and gender isolation.

Leon believes that men have a valuable contribution to make in the lives of young children. He is optimistic about the growing involvement of men in children's care, particularly in the light of the expanded role of fathers:

> I think that perhaps 40 years ago even seeing a man pushing a pram would be seen as strange [laughs] and now you do see men almost like equal, … looking after children. You do have men looking after children, so it actually is changing.

I had the feeling from Leon's openness in our interview that our conversation offered him a rare opportunity to reflect on his choice to cross over the gender line and work in the nursery. Having lived with this decision for 12 years, Leon does not typically expend energy thinking about how he got to where he is now. Towards the end of our talk, he unexpectedly shared with me a particular insight about entering this women's world. He recalled memories of his affirmative childhood experiences 'being around women', including his mum and his grandmother, listening to their conversations. 'I was always happy being in women's company.' These recollections help him understand why he ended up in a female work environment. In the end, Leon's self-confidence prevailed and he resolved to remain in his chosen occupation. This decision has brought tremendous satisfaction to him, the children and their parents.

Men in the British ECEC workforce

In order to deepen my understanding of Leon's work in the nursery, I interviewed Julian Grenier, the Early Years Advisor to Tower Hamlets Council at the time that this research was conducted. He himself worked with young children for many years in London and Sheffield and he recently served on a national workforce, the Nutbrown Review, to examine the qualifications of the UK workforce in ECEC. Thus his perspective was particularly helpful in interpreting my primary data.

Julian referred to the Nutbrown Review into Early Years Provision, in which policies about recruiting men into ECEC were raised. While in 2010 men composed only 1–2 per cent of the ECEC workforce in the UK (Brind *et al.*, 2011: 97), the report suggests that low pay cannot fully explain the phenomenon. The review includes a goal of increasing the participation of men. Professor Nutbrown describes her approach to gender balance:

> I am inclined to think that the more general approach of raising quality and standards through qualifications, establishing clearer career routes and improving the perceived status of the early years workforce will help more men see the value of the profession, and encourage them to consider working with children.
>
> (Nutbrown, 2012: 49–50)

Work in a nursery in England requires some level of qualification for at least 50 per cent of the staff. In state-maintained nurseries such as Mary Sambrook, it is common for all the staff to have a Level 3 childcare qualification, which can be obtained through a one- to two-year course. According to Julian, this qualification is generally thought to be an appropriate track for 'girls who don't do well in school. It is seen as an easy qualification to get'. Because the job is viewed largely as 'emotional work' (Osgood, 2006), it is deemed to be suitable for someone who likes to be with babies and toddlers, even if they lack appropriate training and skills required to care adequately for young children. Beyond the low status of the nursery childcare worker, Julian suggested that an additional deterrent for men is the fear of not being accepted by women colleagues. He was afraid of this himself when he began his first job working with 3–4-year-olds. But he encountered acceptance by all his female co-workers, who taught him the ropes. Because his initial fear had been so intense, Julian believed such anxiety could deter men from choosing such a job. Leon's report of his difficulties with being accepted initially gives validity to Julian's hypothesis.

Julian approaches gender balance with caution. He would prefer to seek the most qualified person for the job instead of using affirmative action favouring men. What counts is a high-quality workforce. But although he would not favour one gender over the other, he actively welcomes male students in work experience placements in the nursery he currently heads. Both Lorraine and Hana were emphatic that they would exercise no gender prejudice in their hiring practice, even though they would like to see more men in childcare.

Anomaly within cultural boundaries

The UK is not a particularly welcoming place for men in childcare. Though academics and early childhood leaders see the need for achieving gender balance, Julian describes this trend as 'ad hoc'. The low percentage of men in the ECEC workforce has persisted over several decades (Cameron, 2001). Although there are attempts in some schools to include more men, they remain the rare exception. Gender balance is not regarded by policymakers as a burning issue. The Nutbrown Review (Nutbrown, 2012), for instance, mentions the need for including more men, but makes no specific recommendations beyond its prime objective to enhance training for early childhood workers across the board. Given the lack of encouragement of men to seek careers in ECEC or aggressive recruitment policies, Leon's job choice seems remarkably bold and invites deeper scrutiny of the reasons for his decision.

The Irish working class culture of East London, in which Leon grew up, made clear distinctions between men's work and women's work. This immigrant group was astutely analysed by Young and Willmott in their classic (1957) study of family structure in East London (1992). They described a matriarchal family structure in which the men who engaged in factory and dock work earned the money. Using whatever funds the husband would give them, the women made most of the important family decisions and raised the children. Leon's thoughts about matriarchal discipline set alongside patriarchal permissiveness echo these findings. Leon spoke in his interview about his personal discomfort with the exigencies of a job that demands strictness alongside caring. In preferring the caring role, he identifies with the traditional permissive male approach that characterizes Irish working class culture, and claims that he has had to learn the strategies of the maternal disciplinarian through his job experience. In Leon's family, his father was largely absent from the household on weekdays, developing his brokerage business. Leon said of his father:

> He was quite a forceful personality if crossed but was and is very kind, generous and loving ... Obviously much of the day-to-day grind (and joy) of bringing me and my siblings up was down to my Mum. She was not a disciplinarian but she inevitably had to do most of the boundary setting when my dad was not around.

The East London society in which he was raised trained the boys to follow their fathers and be the breadwinner who allows his wife to run the household and raise the children. The nurturing side of his father, which Leon encountered at weekends, may have influenced his gentler side as a role model who demonstrates caring as a positive masculine trait.

Leon's unhappy school experience led to a lifestyle as a young adult in which he lurched from one job to another. His decision to complete the A-level in an adult education course was related to his drive to find a steady job. Thus when the significant woman in his life, his long-term girlfriend, found an advert for a childcare training course, he was able to accept her suggestion. Crossing the gender line may seem impossible for many men in his society, but Leon chose to enrol on the course as part of his larger scheme of finding a steady job, which his culture values. His earlier experience as a male minority in the adult education course prepared him for the training for nursery caregivers, where he was again a minority of one. Although he had no intention of working in the caregiver role, he again followed his girlfriend's suggestion to answer the advert for a position at the Mary Sambrook Day Nursery. Leon was surprised to receive an immediate offer, but his girlfriend urged him to take the job. His decision gained approval of his father, who had probably given up on Leon's going into the family business. The support of his girlfriend and family enabled him to make the decision to try working with the youngest children.

I suggest that Leon's ability to cut through cultural gender expectations was related to the fact that the women close to him accepted his choosing a traditionally women's career. Furthermore, Leon had developed a sense of independence from mainstream gender norms. He had already placed himself among nonconformist musicians. Secondly, it could be that his family had watched him drift for 20 years and were so pleased at the prospect of his having a steady job that they were willing to set aside the gender issue.

Leon's trajectory is atypical in that he navigated many waters before settling down, in contrast with Young and Willmott's findings decades earlier, that men in East London reached their maximum earning power by age 20 and tended to remain in their job unless the business closed (1992). Leon's ease with women seems to derive both from his personality – what he calls the gentler side of the male, and from the strong role of women in Irish immigrant society. Although he chose women's work, he has conformed to his culture's gender expectations by leading a heterosexual life, attending football games with the guys and playing in a male band. These cultural markers signal for him a strong masculine identity. The women's work he engages in during the day is balanced by the gender conformity in his private life.

Julian claims that most men who begin working in ECEC eventually move out of the classroom into management. Lorraine adds that this trend is explained by the men's need to support their family by taking better paid positions and thus is not unique to the UK (Cameron, 2001). Leon's decision to remain in the classroom challenges the classic male competitive stance, and the usual hegemonic male drive to move forward in a career track. Leon has found his comfortable niche, made amends for his non-stereotypical gender choice, and seems immune to society's dictate that men must move ahead in their career. He defines himself as a loner, comfortable in the position of being a minority of one. The strong female role models in his life, combined with his gentle personality, allowed him to make an anomalous decision that he has stuck to for 12 years. Although he speculated about transitioning to other work, he has so far done nothing, and it would seem that he will remain a gifted nursery caregiver for the foreseeable future to achieve this goal.

Chapter 8

Reidar Eliassen

Pedagogic Leader, Betha Thorsen Kanvas-Barnehage
Oslo, Norway

'A delicate balancing act'

Reidar's quiet energy permeates the large open space as his charges, aged almost 2, toddle, walk and run to find him, with mutual smiles and open arms. A veteran of 11 years in post at the non-profit and highly prestigious Kanvas Day Care Consortium, Reidar knew from his first day as a fill-in substitute that he had found his calling.

After finishing high school in Hokksund, a small town in rural Norway, Reidar set his sights on professional football, but settled on a course in journalism. The attractions of the big city lured him to Oslo when he was 20. He quickly made friends and began working at a gas station. When a friend who taught in a day care centre asked him to substitute for her, he thought he had nothing to lose. That day was transformative. Reidar was enchanted by playing with the children and enjoyed himself in ways he had never thought possible in previous jobs. By the end of the day, he was asking himself: 'Do I actually get paid for playing with these children?' Recognizing Reidar's intuitive talents with the preschoolers, the director invited him back for continued substitute teaching, and this casual work quickly led to a full-time job as an assistant. Reidar never looked back on his unrealized career as an athlete or journalist, but took to working with children as though this had always been his goal.

All Reidar's friends were positive about his decision, though some of his closest male friends would make 'harmless jokes' from time to time. Despite this banter, he feels they support his working in the day care centre. And his parents wholeheartedly approved of his new career. He continued along this path and completed a bachelor's degree in ECEC, to the delight of his parents that he had seized an opportunity for higher education and professional training. His father had acquired a religious education and worked as a preacher for 27 years, holding major positions in various church organizations.

Backed by family and friends, Reidar is committed to his career. He combines unwavering self-confidence with a passion for working with children. Caring for young children fits his own needs and abilities, and he values his unique contribution to the growth and development of the children under his care. Reidar's enthusiasm is reflected in his assessment of how his professional life has affected him personally: he has learned to resolve conflicts in his own life and to communicate clearly with other people. His attitude to his career choice is wholly positive:

> The humour and happiness is all around, and each day when I'm going to work sitting on the bus I'm looking forward to get[ting] to my job. I know it's not many people who can say that they're looking forward to get[ting] to their job.

Reidar likes to think back on an exceptional man teacher whom he encountered in his first job. This mentor–colleague was a significant source of support and inspiration:

> I could see a young man having fun with the kids playing. He was like a really important role model ... For me it was really motivating to see him there. The adult women didn't play so much with the kids. Actually it seemed like they didn't like to be around kids at all.

Reidar began his career as an aide in the same day care centre where he had substituted on that propitious day, and remained there for six years, beginning a bachelor's degree in early childhood education after the first two. As part of his studies he was placed in an internship in a day care centre affiliated with the Kanvas non-profit organization. His mentor, Oivind Hornslien, convinced him to move to the centre he directed upon completion of his studies. Reidar had worked there for two years when Oivind was invited by the Kanvas organization to open a new centre in Oslo, and brought Reidar with him. The Kanvas Day Care Organization (www.kanvas.no) committed itself to staff its 59 centres with teachers who are representative of society at large, particularly as regards gender balance. Within a year of setting a policy to hire more men, they reached a national average of 18 per cent male staff, increased two years later to 22 per cent. So Reidar seems to have landed in the right place at the right time. At the new centre in Oslo, Reidar followed one group of children for a three-year period, and when they moved on to elementary school, he began with a new group of 1-year-olds. At the time of my visit, Reidar was team-teaching with another pedagogic leader, and altogether they had four assistants for a group of 22 young toddlers. Reidar and his colleague plan to remain with this group for five years, advancing each year with the children until they leave for elementary school.

Reidar's university training was supported by Kanvas, where he first worked as an aide. The centre allowed him to work half-time so he could study, and covered some of his expenses. His experience at college was largely positive. The ten men in the cohort of 80 students were grouped together for 'social support'. Reidar speaks about the significance of this group and in particular the man who became his 'best friend' and now works as a kindergarten teacher. He stresses that 'it was important for me to see another guy being so dedicated to work with kids. I don't think I would have gotten through the school if there were no men there.' One problem he noted was that 'some of the teachers where a bit out-dated'. His experience and expertise have come full circle: Reidar now mentors both men and women interns from the college during their four- to six-week practicum. Once Reidar needed a male role model to spur him forward, and now he is an effective example for others.

Work career

Reidar's style of interaction with the children is based on meaningful personal engagement. Encounters are intentional, generated by mutually agreeable bonds that can be initiated by either party. Reidar approaches these interactions through careful observation, to assess the child's needs in their current stage of physical, emotional, kinaesthetic, cognitive and social development, and he initiates playful contact accordingly. For their part, the toddlers often come to him with a hug or a request to sit on his lap. The resulting play is pleasurable for both Reidar and the child as interactions have a positive emotional tone. Reidar exhibits two modes of interacting with the children: caring and challenging. The caring mode means giving emotional support, physical contact and human warmth. But Reidar also addresses the children's cognitive and social needs, nudging them gently towards more mature language, physical performance and problem-solving. Play occupies centre stage in Reidar's philosophy of working with young children.

A morning in Reidar's toddler room

Reidar's preferred play venue is the floor, where he meets the children eye to eye and hug to hug. Through play, he captures their exact level of interest whether exploring the contents of a cloth bag or the challenges of large rubbery Lego pieces. He can easily lie on his back, curved upward at each extremity like a rocking boat, performing a delicate balancing act with the child. He lifts the toddlers gently into the air and allows them to stretch out above him for a moment. His physical contact involves constant movement and energy, which delights the children. His skill at balancing the children's energy levels with his own extends to carefully weighing the needs of his toddlers against his own ideas of stretching their experience and challenging them with play ideas that are a bit beyond their current level of activity. By recognizing the children's developmental boundaries, he is able to operate within their range of willingness without pushing them too far.

Although he could easily become the focus of attention and lead the children's play, Reidar defers to them and encourages them to lead with their own play ideas. I noted this when observing him play with Vegard while sitting cross-legged on the carpet. The child approached him and sat himself in Reidar's lap. Reidar responded with a hug, as he stretched out on his side with Vegard attached. He tickled Vegard playfully, then sat up as his small friend toddled over to a ball, which he threw to Reidar. Reidar pretended to throw the ball in the direction of Vegard but dropped it behind his back instead. This ball game continued for five minutes, Reidar challenging the toddler with unexpected manoeuvres, which always resulted in Vegard getting the ball. So Vegard initiated the ball play, but Reidar enhanced the game.

His artful and mediated balance was again evident in his response to Linnea, the youngest of the toddlers. She had not quite mastered the skill of walking and when she toddled over to Reidar, she fell at his feet. Reidar extended one finger of each hand, slightly above Linnea's shoulders. Taking the cue, she wrapped her hands around Reidar's extended fingers, raised herself up to standing, released her grip, and toddled on across the room. This illustrates Reidar's sensitivity to the physical, kinaesthetic and emotional needs of the child, which enables him to provide exactly the right scaffolding to enable further growth and development towards the goal the child is striving for.

I also saw Reidar employ careful observation. Whether standing or prone, Reidar constantly scans the vigorous dynamics of the toddler room. Twenty-two children filled a large uncluttered space, energetically involving themselves, their peers and the adults around them in their activity. Reidar was attentive to those who needed help, to those who could benefit from further challenge and to those who were unsuccessful in negotiating the use of a toy with a peer. At first even this seasoned observer could not always discern why he approached a particular child. However, once he began interacting, I could see clearly that Reidar was mediating in situations for the benefit of the child. Reidar's choices were not random but were carefully focused on meeting the needs of the child he approached. His interaction with Emma provided an outstanding example of his unique style of observation and mediation. Emma sat quietly on the floor exploring a cloth bag filled with toys. She was content to reach in and pull out a new toy, and then search for another.

Reidar sat on the floor next to her, watching without interfering. As he moved into her learning space, she reacted with delight at her discoveries. They discussed each extracted object, examining it together, thus extending and enriching the play/learning routine that Emma had established for herself. This dyadic interaction continued for ten minutes, with Reidar giving Emma his undivided attention. Another toddler, Hedda, approached and sat in her caregiver's lap, looking on intrigued. Reidar lifted her from time to time to give her a better view of the bag's contents which were being slowly revealed. Eventually Emma began sharing items from her treasure trove with Hedda. As they began to interact, Reidar's lap was no longer required and only then did he stand up and move on to his next challenge.

Reidar exhibited caring primarily by paying careful attention to the needs of the children. On the morning of my visit, he was emotionally on duty from the first child's arrival at 7.30 a.m. until his shift ended at 3.00 p.m., with a half-hour break in the middle of the day. I never once saw him stop to chat idly with any of the many adults in the toddler room. When parents delivered their child, he conversed briefly with them while focusing his attention on the child.

I watched a situation unfold that, in my opinion, demanded an extended conversation with the mother as well as some concentrated interaction with the child. Although I do not speak a word of Norwegian, I could see that Tiril had extreme separation problems that morning. Reidar took a different tack, standing back and allowing the mother and child to work things out together. When the mother was ready to speak with Reidar, she had quite a bit to say to him and to Tiril. After a full 15 minutes the mother departed, satisfied that Tiril's needs were addressed. Reidar took Tiril in his arms and they made an extended tour of the toddler room, while he stroked her cheek, rubbed her back, and spoke soothingly, pointing out various play options, never pushing her to make a choice. Afterwards, he took her to the sliding glass door through which she could observe various outdoor activities. This demonstration of affection and concern continued until Reidar realized that Tiril might be hungry. He asked her which chair she wished to sit on, and then gently lowered her into the chair next to a low table, brought her a buttered cracker and milk, then squatted to her eye level as she began to eat. Once Tiril was launched with this tempting breakfast, Reidar moved on to attend to other children.

Throughout the morning, Reidar exhibited physical and emotional caring with the children, largely through physical contact. Hugging, holding, lap sitting, bouncing and lifting are his modus operandi. He enhances the physical interactions with dialogue, explanations and questions that delight the children. He is especially concerned about attending to the children's emotional state. Among the many staff in the room, it was Reidar who was most often immediately aware of a child's emotional distress and who shared their moments of delight.

Reidar also exhibited care by attending to the children's physical needs. In preparing for outdoor play on a breezy day, he checked whether a nappy needed changing, put on jackets and changed shoes from indoor to outdoor gear, according to Norwegian custom. He performed each ritual with one child at a time, taking care to give each the attention required. No child was rushed so it required 15 minutes to equip the four children under his care. For Reidar, changing nappies is as routine as tossing a ball. I noticed him from time to time sniffing and, when in doubt, taking a peek to see if a nappy change was required. This he did tranquilly, making conversation against the background of a music box. Reidar enjoys his caring role, whether it involves calming a distraught child, hugging one who wants some physical warmth and contact, or changing a nappy. These caring activities grow out of his concern and affection for the children, and his professional responsibility to provide for their needs *in loco parentis*.

Masculinity in the day care centre

When considering the significance of being a man who works with young children, Reidar's openness about his own masculinity was unusual. He knows that men are expected to engage in rough-and-tumble play with the children, but he does not see himself in this stereotypical role: 'I've never been a rough player myself, I don't do a lot of pretend fighting with the kids, I don't jump up in all the trees, but I always played with the kids.' I asked him if he is expected to do things requiring physical strength such as lifting, carrying, moving and fixing. He unabashedly told me: 'If something practical needs to be done in the kindergarten the adults can more often ask the men … but they don't ask me anymore because they know I can't do any of those things. I'm not that strong.'

In his career in three different centres, Reidar has never experienced rigid gender roles among the staff: 'I've always done the same thing that everyone else does in the kindergarten, I still change nappies and I clean up after a meal. It's important for the kids to see that we all do the same things.' He admits that cultural forces are still at play and that sometimes he does feel gender bias, but maintains that this bias is in his own mind rather than being real. 'Some things can go easier for you because you're a man and some can go harder for you, but I don't think that's something we do on purpose. It's in your consciousness that you just don't think about it but it still happens, even though you're not aware.'

I thought I could follow up on this comment to get Reidar to express some tacit aspects of gender differences. He said he feels that both men and women show more respect to men leaders and listen to directions better when they are given by men. Reidar suggested that the man's presence conveys authority more effectively than the woman's. In a related gender issue, he noted that after consulting with his staff about a sick child, he usually calls the mother to report the illness and reflected that: 'It is something we do because of the history and culture of seeing the mother as the most important caregiver for their child, and I believe that somehow it's still in people's unconsciousness.'

Reidar is keenly aware of preferential treatment in hiring practices:

> I know that being a man in kindergarten I will never have a problem getting a job. You're always popular when you apply for work in a kindergarten. It will be a little easier for a man to get work as a preschool teacher than a woman because the community and everyone wants to have a certain percentage of men working in kindergarten.

In addition to favourable recruitment policies, men are greatly appreciated by the parents. Reidar told me that when prospective parents visit the centre, they often comment on the high number of men caregivers, which they see as beneficial to their young children. 'They think it's important for the kids.' Reidar enjoyed the opportunity of working with other men at the centre. When he began his first job, he had only one male co-worker. In this, his third job, he enjoys the company of several men. 'It's quite easy to be friends with men working in kindergarten because you have many things in common. This is ... something that you might not find among other professionals because [in childcare you work so closely together].'

In his study of male day care assistants' attitudes towards caring, Askland (in press) found them to be 'generous and inclusive'. Not only did the men define their own caring role as showing warmth and empathy, but they also expressed joy in being with children. They encourage independence, instil confidence and push for mastery. While Askland identifies these traits among his male respondents, he hesitates to generalize them to apply to all men in the field. Reidar too discounts the notion of typical masculine traits. He enjoys the variety among the men in his centre and feels no pressure to conform to a particular masculinity dictated from outside: 'We say that if I'm a man it doesn't mean that I have to be like this or like that. We are many men in this kindergarten but we're all different.' His self-confidence as a man among many in a gender egalitarian work environment means that Reidar can be comfortable with his own masculinity as he understands it. He does not need to prove to others that, despite his career choice, he is still a man. As he said: 'I never tried to be a woman before.'

Men in childcare in Norway

My search for a Norwegian male early childhood worker led me to Oivind Hornslien, director of one of the Kanvas day care centres in Oslo. The Kanvas organization (www.kanvas.no) is a non-profit foundation that aims to provide quality childcare throughout Norway. Oivind was interested in my project and eager to connect me with one of his men teachers. He did not have to search widely for a candidate for my research, as 45 per cent of the lead and assistant teachers in his centre are men. This gender ratio has been an aim not only for Oivind but also for the whole Kanvas foundation over the past few years. When the government set a goal of increasing the participation of men in early childhood care from 10 to 20 per cent within ten years, the Kanvas organization set its objective at 30 per cent men in its 60 centres, a goal that it is approaching but has not yet met. Our interview on the day of my visit to the centre focused on issues of recruitment and retention of men in the centre. According to Oivind, the staff should reflect the society so he has made special efforts to include teachers from various ethnicities, religions and sexual orientations: 'I want all kinds of men and women in my kindergarten. We have homosexuals, we have lesbians, we have Muslims, we have Christians, we have people from Africa and everywhere. I mean this is a part of the society we're living in.'

While Muslim immigration is on the rise in Norway, Africans now account for 9 per cent of the immigrant population. Over the past 60 years immigration to Norway has increased from 1.4 to 13 per cent of the total population (Statistisk sentralbyrå, 2013). To increase the number of men in his centre, Oivind follows a national policy that permits him to take affirmative action towards men applying for what is traditionally a woman's job. Working in a day care centre as an assistant is one of the few desirable jobs in Norway that does not require post-secondary training. When he advertises a job for one assistant position, Oivind can receive 60 applications. All men who submit résumés are interviewed, whereas women go through a screening process before they get to the interview stage. In the past, Oivind has been known to choose an inexperienced man over a woman with years of teaching experience if he thinks the man has potential. Oivind expressed pride in the staff he has assembled. He feels that the social interactions at the centre reflect life in the real world: 'I think it's just an extra positive asset to the social interaction at work, I mean ... there is laughter, there is joy, there is fighting, there is disagreement, there's flirting, there's all these things that makes a staff group alive ... so it's only positive.'

Oivind emphasized the unique contribution of men to the children's daily experiences: 'They bring their gender and they bring their way of being and caring for the children. Men are so different. That's why I don't want just one type of guy, I want a spectrum of men.' He reflected that some boys play differently than girls, 'more physical, more running', and suggested that men could possibly meet the needs of the boys better because they allow them to be who they are. He sees a difference between the genders even in terms of their learning: 'Boys have a different way of learning, they have a different way of thinking, and [of] absorbing what they are supposed to learn.' Their behaviour is characterized by *Knoffing* – rough-and-tumble play – but the women are more likely to 'stop them, because it's noisy, it's annoying, and it disturbs their organization.' He also claimed that men are 'a bit more physical in their way of caring' and that women focus more on organizing the children, sitting them at tables, while 'men are more down on the floor, in direct interaction with the children'. An image flashed into my mind of Reidar lying on his back while raising a toddler in the air at arm's length above him, both of them enjoying every second.

Watching Reidar that morning left me with many unanswered questions about physical contact in the caregiver's work, and I used my precious time with Oivind to explore the issue. I wondered if he or the Kanvas organization set boundaries on caregivers' physical contact with the children. Oivind was surprised and replied eloquently:

> [It's] my strong belief, if we only think what's best for children and [their] development, I believe that physical contact with the caregivers is necessary. It's important when they are changing nappies, when they are cuddling, that they say – oh, this is your this and this is your that. This is about learning and development. The children are going to know their bodies and hopefully we are going to send children from the kindergarten who have very confident beliefs in themselves and in their own bodies.

Over the past 20 years, the early childhood community in Norway has paid some attention to children's sexuality (Langfeldt, 1987), which Oivind explained as 'about getting to know your own body'. Following this approach, children are allowed to take off their clothes in the water-play room – the large, tiled space that has taps, large tubs and other equipment that encourages children to explore the sensory-motor experience of water play. Oivind told me that he insists that the caregivers use their own judgement in exercising caution regarding touch and declared: 'We don't run around touching children' and went on to explain:

> I mean, it might just be one word, one sentence from a child saying that – oh no, this blah, blah, blah, touched my – in the kindergarten, and then some alarm bells might start to ring, and of course it would be a huge scandal. ... Even though it might have been totally innocent and normal, so I do think that the staff think about these things.

Although he says that teachers use common sense on the matter of touch, Oivind supports, even demands, that there be normal physical contact between caregiver and child:

> Hugging, caring, they have to do that, otherwise they don't work here, because this is essential. I mean it's the whole base of being able to be a good caretaker ... With the smallest ones, if you don't touch them they die. That's what they need. They need to be touched, to be cuddled, to be lifted, to be tickled. For me, that's maybe the most important basic skill all people working with children need to have is that relationship ... with the kids, to comfort them, to cuddle them, to challenge them.

When I asked about people's suspicions that men who choose to work with young children might be paedophiles, he emphasized that the first priority was to protect children from abuse. He told me that all men and women who apply for work in the kindergartens must, for example, obtain a certificate from the police that they have no record of child abuse. The last time the issue arose was in 1993, when a few men were accused of paedophilia, setting off child-abuse hysteria throughout Norway. Since then things have quietened down completely and, according to Oivind, 'it's not an issue any more'.

Oivind's analysis of the problem is astute. He points out that statistical evidence shows that most abuse happens within families, not in ECEC institutions. He suggested that the reason the issue persisted in the past in spite of the evidence was that men who choose a non-masculine job were automatically suspected of having another agenda. He finds this disturbing and hopes that this will change as it becomes commonplace for men to work in ECEC.

I found Oivind's open-mindedness as a leader in early childcare refreshing and inspirational. His commitment to gender balance fits his larger vision of the childcare centre as a microcosm of the ideal society in which gender equality meshes with values of multiculturalism and respect for children and their families. He views his role as day care director broadly: he has a responsibility for the healthy growth and development of the children and well-being of the adults with whom he works. It was easy to understand why Reidar had chosen to follow Oivind to the centres he directed, once he completed his academic training. Oivind has tremendous respect for Reidar, and Reidar in his daily practice reflects the values that are the basis of Oivind's vision for childcare in Norway.

The centrality of gender equality in Norway

Norway is considered to be a leader among nations regarding gender equality (Norwegian Ministry of Children, Equality and Social Inclusion, 2011), and is placed among the top five of 20 'rich countries' in terms of gender equality as measured by the parental leave policy (Ray *et al.*, 2008). For the past 35 years, the Norwegian welfare state has played an active role in achieving gender equality through legislation and policy reform. The first Gender Equality Act, passed in 1979, was focused on achieving equal status for women in employment. However, the legislation also concerned men working in what were seen as women's professions, encouraging men to work in ECEC. Further legislation was enacted in 1996 to solidify gains in women's employment and fair treatment, as well as benefits such as parental leave that would facilitate women keeping their jobs.

The latest effort for pushing ahead the frontiers of gender equality is the 2014 Action Plan (2011). This document, published by the Ministry of Children, Equality and Social Inclusion, boasts of past achievements along with articulating a commitment to achieving full gender equality in all realms of life: personal, family and in the workplace. Among the stated goals are ensuring fair employment for immigrant women, educating the next generation towards gender equality, and increasing participation of men in kindergartens (birth to age 5) and elementary school. The 2014 Action Plan is far reaching in its reform stance, as apparent in the introduction by Audun Lysbakken, the former Minister of Children, Equality and Social Inclusion, in which he laments the fact that in families it is still women who take the majority of parental leave. While governmental policies have diminished the gender gap through 'adjustable/flexible gender balance thresholds of 40–60 per cent' (Skjeie and Teigen, 2005: 188), women still make up only a small minority in leadership positions in business, with a somewhat larger representation in government.

The gender equality discourse appears central to the national ethos of modern Norway (Menke-Eide, 2012). The government website for gender equality featuring information about the legislative and proactive measures being taken ('Gender in Norway', n.d.) boasts two current tactics being used: 'gender specific actions' and 'gender mainstreaming'. The first strategy is reactive, and attempts to correct existing gender inequalities. Sanctioned by the United Nations Convention on the Elimination of All Forms of Discrimination against Women (CEDAW), measures include a liberal childbirth leave policy for both parents and affirmative action hiring policies. Such procedures involve quotas that regulate job entry into fields characterized by gender imbalances (Teigen, 2006). Gender mainstreaming is proactive, calling 'for the integration of gender perspectives into all stages of policy processes – design, implementation, monitoring and evaluation'.

Norway's national bureau of statistics published a report on gender equality, which includes a variety of issues: family and household, births and children, education, work, wages, time use, and power and influence (Hirsch, 2010). It shows the monitoring of relevant data related to achieving gender equality such as the regional gender equality index, which has been updated every year since 1999. The report indicates an increased reduction in the gaps in labour force participation for women and men and a trend towards equal pay for equal work. In 2008, 71 per cent of women and 77 per cent of men aged 15–74 were in the labour force, a small difference when compared to other developed countries.

Although government policies may account for a large proportion of the gender equality that has been achieved in Norway compared to other countries, Fougner Forde and Hernes (1988) had noted the importance also of economic development and the women's movement and argue that the proactive Norwegian gender equality legislation was both a result of these factors and an expediter of changes towards gender equality.

In their comparison of the gender equality discourses found in Norway and Sweden, Teigen and Wängnerud (2009) conclude that Norwegian culture is characterized by liberal feminism, which is focused on the individual and her claims for equal rights (Bryson, 2003). This ethos stands in sharp contrast to the conflict model of radical feminism in Sweden, which represents a more activist approach. Growing out of the Norwegian liberal feminist approach is an understanding of equality 'in terms of a harmonious, linear process of gradual development', an approach reflected in the multifaceted efforts, both governmental and private, to achieve gender equality as a social goal.

However, there is a clear gender divide in terms of occupational choice, with women still choosing traditional female roles such as kindergarten and elementary school teaching, nursing, secretarial and cleaning. One important legislative initiative to encourage women to join the workforce includes incentives to increase day care services and subsidizing their costs. In 2006, 73 per cent of mothers of young children under the age of 6 were working (Ellingsaeter and Leira, 2006). By the year 2011, 90 per cent of the children age 1–5 were enrolled in some form of organized childcare or kindergarten (Emilsen, 2012).

The increase of women in the workforce has created a shift from the more traditional nuclear family as a norm until the 1980s (Menke-Ende, 2012) to the 'dual-family model' in which both parents work and childcare responsibilities are handed over to the day care centre (Oun, 2012). The state's intervention in family arrangements has been termed 'de-familization' by Edlund (2007), who notes changes in the home engendered by public policy encouraging women to enter the workforce. Despite the vast increase in the percentage of Norwegian women working outside the home, they continue to manage the burden of household chores, childcare and care of elderly parents (Stier and Lewin-Epstein, 2007).

Ellingsaeter and Leira (2006) refer to this phenomenon as 'a situation of gender equality light' (ibid.: 268). A particularly interesting attempt to achieve gender equality at home as well as in the workplace is the work-sharing couples study, conducted in the 1970s and spearheaded by Norwegian sociologists. The 16 couples who participated in this project agreed to share not only the workload outside the home but also child-rearing and domestic chores (Bjornholt, 2009). Results showed improved emotional dealings, attainment of more equal power relations, less stress and better relations with the children. Although 'household chores were largely shared, some traditional gender patterns were found as well' (ibid.: 307). Bjornholt views equality in unpaid work as the next frontier of gender equality.

An important aspect of achieving gender equality in Norway is the drive to increase men's participation in ECEC. The value of men in child-rearing has been recognized and now informs public welfare. In 1996, the government instituted a liberal policy of parental leave upon the birth of a child, which allows women to maintain their income while raising a family and grants rights to return to their job. In 2009, parental leave was extended to 46 weeks with full pay, or 56 weeks with 80 per cent pay, which two-thirds of the women preferred. The financial payment policy encouraging fathers to stay at home with full pay was lengthened to ten weeks and non-transferable. Sixty per cent of fathers availed themselves of the benefit. Norway's higher fertility rate compared to other European countries (1.9 per cent) may be due to the availability of childcare centres and a cash support scheme for parents that makes 'it easier for women to combine a career and children' (Statistisk sentralbyrå, 2010).

The national campaign to attract men into ECEC reflects a steady move towards gender equality. Anders Menka-Eide (2012) compared the response of two societies, Norway and New Zealand, to the paedophilia hysteria that erupted in 1993, when in both countries only 2 per cent of the ECEC workforce consisted of men. While in New Zealand the percentage of men continued to drop after this furore, in Norway it gradually increased over the years. The New Zealand government took no action, whereas the Norwegians began to actively recruit men into the field, heightening public awareness of the importance that men work with young children, and appealing to young men to consider ECEC as a career. This approach led to a steady increase of men in ECEC to its 2010 level of 10 per cent, and an even more promising 14 per cent of all ECEC university students (Statistisk sentralbyrå , 2010). This relatively high rate of men in the ECEC workforce can best be understood in the light of the government's legislative and policy initiatives which prioritize gender equality.

Acceptance by their co-workers can still be an issue. Kari Emilsen is a scholar of gender balance in ECEC at Trondheim University and the former manager of the national Ministry of Education and Research project to recruit men to study and work in the field. She found overall positive attitudes by both men and women childcare workers towards men in the profession. However, when asked if they would like to have more men working in their own centres, there was a drop in affirmative answers. The survey respondents also rejected the notion of having men in the day care centre 'at any price' (Emilsen, 2012). She concludes that more needs to be done to engender supportive attitudes towards men as co-workers.

My investigation shows that the Norwegian government has taken its role in realizing gender equality as a national goal seriously. Whether the national discourse has driven the legislative reform or vice versa, we see a society that is engaged in changing itself for the better. Government, academia and grassroots effort are all involved. The welfare state is proud of its achievements but wants to achieve even more, and increasing men in ECEC is one change that is recognized. Reidar and his director, Oivind, are deeply involved: Oivind through professional development activities on a national level and Reidar on a personal level. But how does the ideological backdrop of equality shed light on Reidar's daily practice and his career trajectory?

Reidar and the gender equality discourse

Reidar was actively recruited to work in the Kanvas organization while maintaining his status as a pedagogic leader acquired in his previous job. He jumped on board in between the second and third waves of gender equality policy reforms in Norway. The inclusive work environment of the day care centre permitted and possibly encouraged his female friend to suggest that he try out working for one day with the children. This open environment enabled Reidar to agree, and to presume – as she did – that men could do this kind of work and do it well. In organizational terms, the female director recognized Reidar's talent, kept him on as an untrained assistant, and encouraged him to study in a bachelor's programme in ECEC. She offered him promotion to pedagogic leader while he studied. Driven by a personal ideology of gender balance, an organizational drive to increase the percentage of men on staff, and a national push towards more men in female professions, Oivind made an attractive offer to the novice teacher he had mentored in his studies. Oivind's offer turned out to be an important step in Reidar's career trajectory, enabling him to continue receiving the benefits of Oivind's leadership and vision. For his part, Reidar morphed from being a drifter from the hinterlands seeking his fortune in the city, to a sound childcare professional who achieved successful practice in the centre and a bachelor's degree in ECEC. Reidar not only gained professional knowledge through his studies but also stature in the day care centres where he worked and in the eyes of his parents, who were pleased to see him earn a higher education degree.

The support from his director and co-workers was echoed in the positive feedback Reidar received from the parents of the children with whom he works. The national policy to encourage professionalization of childcare workers enabled him to continue working 50 per cent at the day care centre while studying half time, and receiving tuition and living subsidies. Thus we see a society that has scaffolded a meaningful career for Reidar in working with children.

Reidar's success is an example of the outcomes of the gender equality project of Norwegian society over four decades. His career trajectory is a casebook study of what policymakers in Norway have been trying to accomplish through their various welfare reforms, positive actions and mainstreaming. The governmental affirmative action policy allowed Kanvas to hire Reidar instead of a more qualified woman, had one applied. That Reidar was placed together with ten other men in his college training programme meant that their mutual support enabled them to successfully negotiate a largely female environment. The decision of the day care organization to support his studies by offering him a lightened workload and a partial scholarship was mirrored by the support network within the college itself. The generally positive attitude of Norwegians towards gender equality in all professions was reflected in the enthusiasm of the parents about having a man care for their young children. All these favourable feelings bolstered the formal aspects of the gender equality network that brought Reidar into the system and kept him there.

However, the individual influences his own trajectory. Reidar is a person with a strong sense of himself as a man. He has freed himself from traditional male hegemonic expectations and normative references and his role model is another man working with young children, whom he encountered in his first job and in his studies. Reidar says he is not particularly strong physically and does not enjoy rough-and-tumble play. Although he gets along easily with the female staff, he particularly enjoys male company and appreciates having other men around. His quiet and gentle side fits the caregiving role he has carved out for himself. It appears that Norwegian society has created a comfortable space for a man whose masculinity is well suited to caring for young children, and that in turn Reidar has found the niche that promotes his positive image of himself as a man.

One of the primary arguments Norwegian gender activists use in their drive to increase men's participation in ECEC is that men make a unique contribution to the care of young children. Reidar's daily practice provides exemplary support for this argument. His contribution to the care and education of the children is grounded in his sensitivity to their needs, his ability to respond, his leadership capabilities in his team, and his quiet energy which sets the tone for his entire group.

To say that these features represent all men or all Norwegian men would be misleading. As Reidar has stated, there are many kinds of men in the centre, indicating that diversity is both positive and healthy. The contribution of men is to be found among their diverse masculinities as well as their respect for and interest in children, which equals that of the women caregivers. Norwegian society has openly invited men to join in the task of raising the next generation of young children and through its agents at Kanvas the society has openly embraced Reidar as a current and future leader in this endeavour. In return, he has openly embraced the children in his care, contributing uniquely to their development and to the strengthening of the society which continues to nurture him as an early childhood caregiver.

Chapter 9

Looking inward – looking outward

Now that we have an understanding of these remarkable ECEC educators, I want to compare and contrast their stories. My subjects are not a scientifically representative sample of men in the profession, neither in their own countries nor in the international arena. As explained in chapter 2, they were recruited through personal networks. Despite the seemingly random nature of this selection, there was strict logic to my method. First of all, I was looking for men who were committed to the ECEC profession and who had proven this commitment by their long service. Secondly, I wanted men who had undergone some formal training, not dilettantes who like to play with little children. Thirdly, I chose teachers who were highly regarded by their supervisors. This allows me to compare them using multiple parameters. Such analysis offers insights from an international perspective and deepens our knowledge of the breadth and depth of the experience of men who choose to work with young children over an extended period of time.

The comparison in this chapter parallels the structure of the six narrative chapters, which each focused on one of the men. We can enjoy a broader cultural overview of the issues raised about each of them and gain insight into both the differences and the commonalities among them. The analysis suggests new categories for thinking about salient issues that recur time and again in the research literature.

The comparison consists of ten sections, each relating to one issue in the men's personal and professional experience over the years. A unique feature of this book is the thick description (Schon, 1983) of the work the men did in their setting. I pay attention to the issue of physical contact between caregiver and child because of its importance in the gender balance discourse. The comparative analysis ends with the metacognitive views of the teachers on two issues that arose frequently in our conversations: their attitudes about the differences between men and women as caregivers and ECEC teachers; and their views of their own masculinity. While one could write a book about each of the ten topics, a few pages on each topic will have to suffice. I end this concluding chapter with a consideration of the theoretical implications, suggestions for further research and some practical recommendations for ECEC decision-makers.

Entering and leaving the profession

In their study of male entry into female-dominated jobs, Williams and Villemez (1993) differentiate between 'seekers' and 'finders'. The 'seekers' are men who actively pursue a career in a female-dominated profession, while 'finders' end up in such jobs unintentionally through an invisible trapdoor. They reject Jacobs's (1993) model of the revolving door, stating that their quantitative data do not support the claim that men, by and large, enter these jobs out of expedience and leave when better opportunities arise. Among the six teachers in my study, only Benny and Eli could be categorized as 'seekers' while the other four might best be described as 'finders', as they entered ECEC through an invisible trapdoor. Eli made a conscious decision to study ECEC after leaving the army, following the 'pathways of his heart'. Benny made a mid-career decision to change jobs because of his extreme dissatisfaction with his job and his search for meaning and significance in his work. Reidar falls somewhere within the continuum. As he reflected, it only took him one day of substituting for a friend in a day care centre to realize that he had found his calling, and it had been totally unplanned. Elton and Levien share similar paths towards their careers in ECE, as both intended to prepare themselves academically for a teaching career with young adolescents (and for Elton, a baseball coaching position). Each had been placed in a kindergarten class for their teaching practicum. Elton had remained for 27 years, and Levien had continued to work with young children for five years. Leon stands alone at the end of the continuum. Until age 26, he had not found a satisfactory job. An advert for a nursery caregiver training programme triggered his girlfriend's imagination, and she recommended that he try it out. A newspaper advert was also a catalyst for Benny; but he found and responded to it on his own initiative. For all six men, the way into the profession does not correlate with the men's decisions to remain. Whether they intentionally sought the job or not, all incorporated their work with young children into their professional identity and chose to remain in the field.

The revolving door model fits the trajectory of Eli and Levien, both of whom planned to enhance their standing by moving up the career ladder. Eli loves working with young children, but his ambitions for upward mobility have led him to consider transforming his physical classroom into a science-oriented magnet programme that would provide enrichment for visiting kindergarten classes in his region. Having mastered the art of setting up and teaching a class of kindergarteners, he is eager for further challenges within early childhood education that do not involve having his own group of children. Levien is interested in moving from teaching into school administration. He knows that to do so he will need to accumulate experience in teaching higher-grade levels, a prospect that attracts him.

Like Eli, Reidar envisions becoming involved in the professional development of teachers. He has already begun to mentor student teachers, and he imagines travelling around Norway to lecture about ECEC issues. Reidar is five years younger and a bachelor, whereas Eli has three children. Reidar seems to be in no hurry to implement his plan, while Eli is eager to take advantage of every opportunity and to create his own. When I asked them to imagine where they will be in ten years' time, each of these men breathed deeply and sighed as they considered their approaching middle age. Eli, Levien and Reidar all planned to move up the hierarchy but not out of ECEC. Similarly, Benny, Elton and Leon all plan to remain in the classroom with young children, a profession they have grown to love.

The family and friendship network at play

Men who choose to work with young children might be considered to be outliers, people whom Malcom Gladwell (2008) defines as 'men and women who do something out of the ordinary' (ibid.: 9). Gladwell examines external, structural factors that might explain the success of these unusual individuals. The six men in my study did something out of the ordinary when they chose to work with young children. Four of them spoke about this aspect of their career decision and all four of them had the backing of family members and, in some cases, friends. While their parents were surprised by their son's career decision, all offered some form of approval. The four men described the positive reactions from their parents in both instrumental and affective terms. Reidar received 'a most wholehearted response' and said that his parents always thought that he would do well working with people, be they adults or children. So his decision fitted with their expectations. Levien's parents looked to the future, telling him: 'If you are happy, it's ok. The best way to do your job is that you are happy about it, because you will keep on doing it.' Elton received an even more instrumental response: 'My parents weren't keen about the kindergarten (job) placement. But in a tight job market, they gave a nodding approval. They thought it was cute.' Leon's mother was happy to see him 'settling down', since, as she put it, 'at least it was a job'. His father, on the other hand, offered support characterized by 'a few question marks related to it being a job more associated with females'. Neither Eli nor Benny mentioned their parents' reactions, possibly because they made their career decisions as mature adults with a successful work record, Eli as a combat officer in the Israeli army and Benny in international customer service.

The responses of friends were somewhat gendered. The four men who spoke about their friends' reactions described their female friends as all being very 'supportive'. Their male friends' responses were more varied but consistently negative. Levien said that his men friends criticized his decision, 'pointing out the low salaries teachers earned'. Reidar said his men friends challenged him, while 'the women understood'. Elton encountered the most negative response: his college friends teased him. Leon reported that all his friends were supportive. He remembers them showing interest 'in how I was doing'. But when socializing with his buddies he rarely volunteers information about his work, which indicates some concern over how this information might be received. The generally negative response of the men has been identified as gender protocol that is typically used to construct gender barriers to maintain masculine hegemony (Williams and Villemez, 1993). However, the positive responses of the women created a balance, a dissonance that allowed them to pursue a decision that matched their dispositions, notably their interest in caring and a desire to be a child again.

The personal ethos of caring

The men in this study expressed their personal ethos of caring (Noddings, 2005; King, 1998) more through their relationship with the children in their group or classroom than through their own narratives. My observations in the day care centres and kindergartens revealed a variety of caring modes but all focused on meeting the needs of the child rather than their own needs or the requirements of the curriculum. With the youngest children, caring had a physical manifestation – touching, hugging, holding and speaking gently. As toddlers are often stressed by separation from the parent, it was no surprise that I observed both Leon and Reidar dealing with a child crying because their parent had just left the day care centre. Each had lifted the distressed child and begun walking around the room, enabling the child to view things from a different perspective. Once the crying ceased and the tears dried, the caregivers found a suitable activity in which the child was willing to engage. Both men demonstrated empathy and compassion by easing the stressful moment in transition from home to centre. The caring by the kindergarten teachers was evident by their verbal and physical response to the children's stress and their nurturing of children's curiosity.

Although overt physical affection is not his primary mode, Benny's immediate words of comfort and a light pat on the head went a long way to communicate his caring for a girl who had inadvertently banged her head on the wall. Likewise, Levien's placing two children in his lap at the morning meeting echoed the way the two teachers of toddlers carried around a distressed child at morning drop-off. Eli noticed a socially isolated child and would sit and eat with her at the snack table, acting on his empathy. In all these cases, the men showed awareness of the children's emotional needs and they reacted sensitively to help them overcome their difficulty and move forward.

Besides the response to emotional stress, the teachers showed caring in their day-to-day work in routine activities. Elton's body language revealed his caring, as he leaned in to the children when they worked on their literacy tasks. He also made intense eye contact, creating what he calls 'intimacy'. Showing genuine interest in their work, he carefully examined each child's product and asked challenging questions.

Levien crafted his individualized instruction for each child according to her self-selected task. He lightly enfolded the child in his arms, allowing her ample freedom, to model the desired solution and to encourage her to try this solution on her own. Eli also physically encompassed the child who was working at a counter preparing the lizard's food. He stood behind the child and reached around on both sides, showing how small to cut the vegetables. Benny likewise focused attention on the children who required special attention on the playground by tailoring an impromptu device with ropes, logs and planks for each. The physical presence, the intense focus and the ability to create challenges are to these caregivers and teachers all important components of caring.

In her pioneering work on caring as an essential characteristic of the way women construct social reality, Noddings (2005) delineated critical features of the caring professions. In an earlier work Noddings (2003) claimed that teaching is essentially a caring profession, in which the teacher (the one caring) focuses her energies on the students (the cared for) (King, 1998: 13). Empathy is a primary element in these relationships. In the descriptions of the expressions of caring among the six men in this study, it appears that they all view their work first and foremost as acts of caring, responding to the emotional needs of the child and to their cognitive requirements. King (1998) studied men who teach in elementary schools and found that his subjects had adapted an ethic of caring at some cost to themselves. For example, when they 'cared about' the children by helping them physically, they were expected to do so with 'authority, force and discipline', a position that his subjects categorically rejected. My subjects, on the other hand, were expected to 'care about' the children with love, kindness and physical contact.

Articulating meaning in work with young children

When they spoke about their personal philosophy of working with young children, some of the men mentioned returning to their own childhood. The most articulate description of this desire came from Benny in his explanation of his mid-career decision to train as a kindergarten teacher. 'The little child in me' is Benny's ideal, and he feels that through his interactions with the children he can discover that child. He aims to see the world through the child's eyes. Leon calls the world of childhood 'a magical time'. He understands his playing with the children to be in some way a throwback to his own childhood. Levien's intense focus on children's curiosity is based on sharing in their wonder and experiencing with them their curiosity about the world.

Another major theme intertwined with the desire to return to childhood is the notion of respect for the individual child. Reidar's work assignment entails remaining with the same group for five years, which fits his philosophy focused on appreciating each child's development over time. By interacting with the children, he has also learned about himself and his relationship with others, including adults. Eli's respect for the child grows out of his commitment to seeing each child as an independent learner. He talks about sharing his authority with the children, particularly as he supports their creating a suitable learning environment. Levien's Montessori training leads him to focus on the individual as a decision-maker about his own learning. Benny honours children's decision-making by engaging them in learning tasks and playing with them according to their lead. He describes his role as one of authority alongside friendship: 'It's like a partnership'. Elton's philosophy of mutual respect echoes that of Benny. Elton understands that he must earn the children's esteem through significant one-to-one contact and by treating them respectfully both as individuals and as a group. Leon's sense of respect shows up more in his style of interaction than through his discussion of educational principles. He honours their decisions about what to eat, where to play, and how to manipulate toys. Because these men are intensely interested in children and childhood, they naturally respect them. The desire to return to childhood and the self-imposed standard of respect for the children under their care are the two formative qualities of their professional identity.

Looking inward, looking outward

A teacher's identity is complex and is composed of interrelated dimensions (Day and Kington, 2008). The professional identity component relates to standards of practice in the profession. The situated local identity refers to the specific stakeholders who influence what happens in a particular classroom.

The personal dimension exists outside the classroom and is tied to family, friends and community. The men in this study strongly identify with their work in ECEC. At one extreme Reidar is quite pleased with his commitment to remain with the same group from toddlers to 5-year-olds. On his morning bus ride to the centre, he thinks about how happy he is to be going to work in a profession he loves. He compares himself to those less fortunate, who cannot claim such pleasurable thoughts about their impending working day. He has striven to become more professional by earning a bachelor's degree in ECEC and by continuing his professional training through opportunities at the centre. Benny shares Reidar's enthusiasm for the job and the centrality of the profession to his self-image. His pride in his professional skills surfaced when he showed me a weekly planning sheet and written records monitoring the children's individual development. His wholehearted commitment to children is apparent through his intensive connection with the children throughout the working day. His mid-life career change to ECEC was driven by his search for personal meaning. He has married a kindergarten teacher. These elements point to a positive professional identity. Leon occupies the other extreme. He is confident about his decision to work as a nursery caregiver, yet separates the day-to-day work at the centre from other aspects of his life. The clarity of his decision is witnessed by his 12 years of uninterrupted work at the same centre, and his compartmentalization is evidenced by his interest in music, football and friends, and also his lack of ambition to move upwards to an administrative position in the centre.

The other men fall somewhere between these two. Eli propels himself forward by seeking opportunities to advance his career. While putting heart and soul into his kindergarten learning environment, he has taken two educational initiatives to achieve advancement: earning a master's degree in informal education and completing a mentoring course at a local education college. Working directly with young children is what he does now, but he is open to other possibilities should prospects present themselves. His view of himself as an early childhood educator extends beyond the boundaries of the kindergarten class into other venues as well.

Early in the process of forming their own professional identities, Levien and Elton each identified a paradigmatic female kindergarten teacher whom they emulated and measured themselves against. For Elton, the model kindergarten teacher was his mentor in his first student teacher placement. He described her thus: 'She wore a linen skirt which never got dirty even though she did messy art projects with the children, and she was very "motherly".' It took him several years to construct his own self-image to compete with and replace this paragon. Levien states openly that he is not the 'ultimate kindergarten teacher', who is in his view embodied in the caring and protective female teacher in the classroom next to his. He has built his professional identity on the basis of being tough, with a soft underbelly, and humorous too. A common thread running through these various descriptions of professional identities is the men's coming to grips with their own masculinity in the light of their choice to engage in women's work, discussed later in the chapter. First, I present a comparison between the teachers' professional practices.

Face to face with parents

Early childhood educators share the child-rearing role with parents, usually with their consent. Schools and centres vary in the extent to which they take account of parental opinion in the placement of a child with a particular teacher. For the man entering the profession, parental objection can prove daunting, while for the veteran teacher, parental approval enhances work satisfaction. The teachers in this study all experienced positive relationships with the parents of the children in their care. Benny and Reidar both spoke of encountering scepticism among some of the parents at first; but noted how their fears 'evaporated' over time. Eli added that once parents got to know him 'face to face', they adopted a positive attitude towards him, and he has enjoyed the backing of all the parents for some years. When confronted with parents' fears, Benny did not let them get in his way. Instead he invited parents to observe him in the kindergarten, gave them his phone number, and encouraged dialogue. His strategy earned feelings of acceptance, respect and trust.

Although Leon claimed that parents were '99 per cent positive', a very few objected to his changing their child's nappy. Levien barely understood my question about parental acceptance. Instead of answering me directly, he referred to one parent who informed him that her daughter was afraid of men and preferred a woman for a teacher. Levien helped the child overcome her fear and established a favourable relationship with her and her parents. Elton said that the school district used him to attract parents to an elementary school that was losing enrolment. He claimed that the feeling among parents was that a man could achieve discipline and work with behaviourally challenged boys better than a woman. Over the years he has built his reputation around an image that children are safe and happy in his class, and that a male role model in the classroom is good for children. Going one step further, Reidar reported that prospective parents at his centre are happy to learn that their child will be cared for by a man because they think that it is important to 'get role models from both genders'.

Common practice

Although the men all grew up in different countries and cultures, they revealed many shared characteristics in their practice. While these teaching methods may be considered as best practice by early childhood experts, I suggest that they are a conglomerate that may contribute towards defining men's particular contribution to the profession. Many women who work with young children exhibit the same traits. My task here is not to compare men and women early childhood workers, but to define how the men work in common ways across cultures, national borders and continents.

Playing with the children was an important part of the day. The teachers play not only because they know that this is how the children learn, but also because they enjoy playing. Their eyes glimmer when they stretch out on the floor to join in a construction project (Levien) or toss a ball in an unexpected direction for the toddler to retrieve (Reidar). Jointly with the children they explored the wonders of water, trying out different ways of pouring and seeing what happens (Leon), worked together on a Lego construction (Benny) or played a card game (Eli) at a table, all engaging with the children as equals.

These incidents represent pleasurable modes of interaction and bolster the desire of some of the teachers to revisit their childhood. In their play as equals they honour the child's way of doing things rather than imposing their own ideas. Leon encouraged the 2-year-olds at the water table to experiment freely. He allowed them to err, to spill, to try out impossible ideas though he knew that the water would often not reach its intended goal. His playful guidance stands in contrast to caregivers who might view these children's actions as clumsy or unsuccessful. Leon also tried out his inventions, enjoying the results from his own trials as much as those of the children. Benny accepted the children's Lego constructions as they formed them. While suggesting his own playful ideas, he was happy to accept the children's decisions about how to create the intended construction, no matter if it fell short of adult expectations. The products were the result of playful dialogue in which the children led and Benny participated almost as a peer.

The men often relinquished their own decision-making authority beyond the play context in other venues. By shrinking their own power, they broadened the possibilities for the children to act on notions of their own world, thus enhancing their sense of efficacy. Eli encouraged the children to plan the end-of-year party by choosing the content of their presentation to the parents. Reidar illustrated this principle beautifully by sitting on the floor with a child for 20 minutes as she explored a bag of toys. As she pulled each one out of the sack and examined it, he observed and reacted to her lead.

The teachers often used playful interactions to foster higher-order thinking among the children, opening new possibilities, looking at a phenomenon from a different perspective, encouraging alternative explanations, and generating and investigating hypotheses. Benny, for instance, mediated with two boys who wanted to cut out a pair of spectacles from paper. After encouraging them to solve their problem of where to insert the scissors into the paper he wore the spectacles in various ways, thereby showing the boys additional possibilities for their creation. Elton's literacy exercise required his young students to think about the emotional impact of various words in order to determine when to punctuate with an exclamation mark. He playfully helped them vocalize various adjectives according to their impact on the listener. Often he challenged a child's suggestions, asking: 'Can you think of an even stronger word?' Levien worked intensively with his students at a station for preparing bubble blowers out of wire, encouraging original solutions to the problem of how to create different kinds of bubbles with different wire configurations. All the men gave the impression that they enjoyed pushing the frontiers of the children's cognitive capabilities with every interaction, structured to unstructured.

Among the pedagogic values the men demonstrated through their interactions with the children was the importance of educating for independence. This was obvious in the four kindergarten classes, but also in Leon's toddler room. Elton encouraged children to complete the literacy and maths tasks he had assigned and demonstrated on their own. Rather than micromanage each child's work, he equipped them with tools for problem-solving, thus enabling them to work independently and to help one another. Eli's style of encouraging independence included offering children responsibilities for aspects of managing the classroom. He placed the animals' care in their hands, including feeding and cleaning cages. Children learned the tasks and then carried them out on their own, with minimal guidance from Eli.

Levien's focus on independent work may draw on the Montessori philosophy that builds on the learner completing self-selected tasks according to predetermined routines. Levien applied this approach in his sensitive mediation, honouring the child's independent thinking and choice about how to proceed. He also encouraged children to initiate their own projects using open-ended materials provided in the classroom. Benny took independent decision-making a step further, setting up a planning board on which the children placed a symbol of where they wanted to play the next day.

With toddlers, independence takes a different form. Both Leon and Reidar encouraged the children to freely choose where they wanted to play, and with whom. While many of these decisions seem random, the caregivers actively supported the children's choices as a way of building their independence. Such autonomy frees the teacher to move from child to child, group to group, mediating and emboldening them to further initiatives.

The 'charisma' of all six men is well described by the dictionary definition of the term: 'A personal magic of leadership arousing special popular loyalty' (Merriam-Webster Online, 2014). Using the word 'magic' would seem natural to the men who employ the term to describe their work. Benny has formulated his email address as: magicben@ ... And Leon claims that the world of childhood he wants to enter is 'magical'. When Benny plays his guitar and the children dance spontaneously and freely, he seems to be performing a kind of magic. He turns a routine activity into an exciting and creative event in which he is involved as much as the children. For the toddlers in Leon's care, he is the centre of energy, the caregiver they choose to follow in the play yard. His special brand of leadership flows from his attention to the children and includes suggestions of play venues and responses that spark interest and imagination.

Eli expresses his leadership by sharing his authority, developing a sense of trust between the children and himself, so making it worth their while to listen to him. Levien runs a very relaxed and quiet class. When he needs the children's attention, he raises his voice slightly above the routine mumble – and the children stop and listen. Elton has a reputation in the Corvallis schools as a strong disciplinarian. While I witnessed total obedience among the children, this was a well-oiled classroom organization based on cooperation and mutual respect. The children followed Mr K's requests because of their awareness that he cares for each individual. For example, his leaning in to the child and establishing eye contact indicates a leadership style that is magical in its own right. The three other caregivers on Reidar's team sense that he is in charge, as do the children. He displays quiet enthusiasm for working with the children, and they follow his lead. Charisma is a shared trait among these six men, an attribute that sets them apart as a unique group of early childhood educators.

How the teachers see men's and women's caregiver roles

My findings revealed a constellation of four characteristics common to the subjects: engaging in play, fostering independence, promoting thinking and a charismatic style of leadership. These constructs share an empirical base because they are drawn from observations and triangulated with what the teachers say about their own teaching and caregiving. In addition to speaking about themselves and their teaching, they spoke at length about how they distinguish men's and women's work with young children. While the reader may not identify with some of the teachers' views, it is crucial to bring their voices to the discussion of gender. Furthermore, the traits that I claim to characterize these men's attitudes and practice may not be exclusive to men, rather they may be viewed as best practice in ECEC. However, when the men view these traits as male, I present their construction of gender in an attempt to capture who they are and what they represent as men working with young children. Their perspectives on the distinctions between men and women ECEC practitioners are followed by their supervisors' views on the topic.

The major themes in the male–female dichotomy include: how teachers of each gender help children respond to stress, how men and women express caring differently, variances in leadership and authority, preferred activities, and the global or overall image of male and female ECEC workers. When I asked the men to tell me how they viewed differences between men and women in the field, they often interpreted my question by comparing themselves with their female colleagues. Their answers reflect their views as generalizations only to the extent to which they saw themselves as representative of men in the profession – which was not always easy to discern.

For Benny, Eli and Levien the true test of the differences between male and female ECEC teachers can be found in their responses to children under stress when there is a real or perceived injury. Benny compared his reactions to the emotionally indulgent responses of his female colleagues, claiming that women focus on the injury while he focuses on building resilience. He suggested that women reinforce children's emotional displays by focusing on them excessively, whereas he supports positive growth and development by addressing the injury objectively and encouraging the child to go back and try again. Similarly, when a child hurt himself both Eli and Levien encouraged them not to fear the sight of blood, but rather to use the opportunity to learn to be strong in the face of pain. As toddler caregivers, Leon and Reidar routinely address stress in a gentle manner, so displayed no gender differences in this respect, believing that it would help foster resilient children in the end.

Achieving discipline was claimed to come more naturally to men than women. Elton believed that classroom management is easier for men because of the paternal role model and Eli suggested that men by nature project authority due to their self-certainty. Levien called his approach 'direct', cutting to the quick and thereby establishing the man's authority over the children. Reidar suggested that men, women and children all listen more readily to men than to women, thus gainsaying the customary Norwegian liberalism.

Several of the teachers mentioned that a male voice is a natural projection of authority, seeing it as an added advantage for men in their position with children.

Although I did not observe the men encouraging children to engage in acts of daring during my visits, Eli and Levien both told me how they embolden the children to try out physical challenges that women view as dangerous. Both indicated that this is typical of men teachers and were proud of their support for children following their inclinations to climb high and jump far. They felt it a restriction on the children's development to suppress their need for performing such physical feats. Daring melds into another male activity: rough-and-tumble play. Levien was the only teacher who indicated his affinity for sports and gymnastics over music and dance, which could be interpreted as expressing conventional gendered preferences. He spoke of enjoying rough-and-tumble play activities in which he constantly needs to set limits for the children.

Some of the men made a distinction between themselves and female colleagues in the domain of caring. They perceived their caring as differing from that of women. Despite his endless demonstrations of caring on a physical level with the children in the nursery, Leon claimed that caring comes naturally to women, and has to be learned by men with great effort. Levien said that he does not identify with women's style of 'caring and protecting', indicating what for him is a core distinction between men and women. Like Leon, his claims belie his behaviour, which is replete with incidents of sensitive care for the children in his kindergarten.

I conclude this section by comparing the ways Levien and Reidar see themselves vis-à-vis women who work with young children. In Levien's interview, a major recurring theme was toughness. For Levien being tough means being a man, in contrast to women, who are soft and caring. Reidar, on the other hand, used the term 'gentle' time and again to describe his work with the children. He saw little difference between his gentle side and that of the women with whom he works. Leon also spoke of the 'gentler side' of his personality, and suggested that women could appreciate that aspect of his personality more than men.

Whereas there was broad consensus between the six men about common practice, no such consistency was found in their attitudes about differences between men and women as ECEC workers. At most, I found three men who expressed similar ideas, although these were nuanced with shades of meaning. The discrepancies between practice and belief reveal the distancing the men tend to place between their ideal selves and their behaviour in the classroom. While the constellation of common practice may represent gender preferences, it could be that their vision of how men behave has limited scope. For example, Leon in his 12 years of work in the nursery has yet to meet another man who fills the same role as nursery caregiver. Given their meagre experience in working with other men in ECEC and being in a tiny minority, these teachers and caregivers are hard put to extract generalities about men and women in the field. Benny is the exception to this rule, as he worked with 25 other men teaching kindergarten in the Basel schools before taking his current job. The others did not try to construct generalities about gender differences but compared themselves to their female colleagues and tried to generalize from that limited perspective. This comparison of self to others in their immediate work vicinity leaves us with a very personal picture of how they perceive themselves as men working in a woman's profession. Their perceptions are most likely coloured by their masculine identity and their need to protect it through outer symbols and through their behaviour. Before moving on to the topic of masculinity, I present a broader perspective by examining the issue of professional gender differences from the point of view of the directors and supervisors of the men in this study.

The supervisors' views added another layer of understanding to the way the men see themselves in comparison to women. As with the teachers, there was little agreement about gender differences. Rather, each one offered a unique view. One trait mentioned by several of the supervisors was the energetic nature of the men's interactions with children, compared to the women's somewhat more 'cerebral' outlook. Oivind and Lorraine both mentioned men's preference for rough-and-tumble play over quieter activities. Lorraine noted that children like to wrap themselves around Leon's legs, almost like a climbing structure. Oivind went on to explain that boys need the physical attention of the men who care for them because the boys themselves have a need for active physical play. He claimed that men understand and honour the children's (and particularly the boys') physical needs, making a place for such activities in their lives.

Eva noted men's preference for more active sports, while the women chose playground games that are more stationary, such as jump rope. Physical positioning in the day care room also differs. Oivind, who had worked in the role of caregiver before becoming a director, described how the many men in his centre tend to choose the floor as a venue for interacting with the children. He described the women as 'organizers' who prefer to sit at tables while engaging the children in activities. Eva has worked with several men teachers in her Montessori school. She too mentioned men's proclivity for active sports, but said that men are 'thinkers' and women are 'doers'. When probed further she explained that men tend to reflect on situations while women are more likely to make quick and intuitive decisions. Ziona, the state inspector of Eli's kindergarten, thought differently. She concluded that men handle children's interpersonal conflicts in a rather decisive manner whereas women are likely to see shades of grey. These diametrically opposed viewpoints would have made for an interesting conversation between Ziona and Eva. Lacking the means to achieve such dialogue, I suggest that Ziona is referring to a Middle Eastern trait of men who see themselves as dominant actors while women take a more reflective and passive role. Perhaps Eva represents a more Western perspective that places men in a thoughtful role and women as more impulsive. Denise, the principal in Elton's elementary school, concluded that men tend to stay away from 'touchy feely things'. Her remark was echoed by Benny who reflected on his formal training as a kindergarten teacher: 'Touch me, feel me – bah! That's not for me.'

I conclude this section on views of gender differences by looking at the aesthetics of the classroom. Ziona claimed that men have little interest in the appearance of their classroom. This judgement proved to be a backhanded compliment to the men who have worked under her supervision, who prefer to focus on the needs of children over decorating walls. Elton related how his first principal gave him two days' paid leave from work in order to visit properly decorated classrooms in the school district, in hopes that the experience would improve his attention to the physical learning environment.

It is no surprise that my question about the gender differences among staff prompted a wide array of answers from the supervisors I interviewed. These leaders have experience with only a few men, the one exception being Oivind who has achieved 45 per cent male staff in his centre. Two further factors might affect how these differences are viewed. One is the cultural lens through which my subjects are looking at the phenomenon and the other is the phenomenon itself that may differ according to social norms. So the variation in the views on differences between men and women in the ECEC workforce sheds light on the gender norms in each society. These norms are challenged by men who cross the gender boundary by choosing to work with young children.

Multiple masculinities: 'I've never been a woman.'

Men in ECEC confront the ever-present reality of being surrounded by women in their work, a situation that causes them to constantly re-examine their masculine identity. Connell (2005) asserts that men construct their own masculinity partly through responses of others to their appearance and partly through their own actions. This paradigm is borne out in my data from the interviews and observations. While none of the men spoke directly about their own masculinity, it was possible to deduce some level of thematic unity among them through their appearance, their actions in the classroom or day care room, and through their comments about related issues that they raised in the interviews.

The similarities in dress between four of the teachers was uncanny. Only Elton and Eli did not come to work in jeans, T-shirt and trainers. In response to the cool Norwegian climate, Reidar added a flannel shirt and wool stocking cap to this uniform. Their informal garb enabled the men to sit comfortably on the floor, engage in messy art projects, and play actively with the children. Although jeans and T-shirt might be viewed as a non-gendered dress code, this was not the case in the school and day care contexts I observed. The women wore skirts or jeans with a feminine top. Thus the men's chosen outfit conveyed a male image that set them apart from their female colleagues. Their dress seemed natural and probably matches the clothing they wear elsewhere. Elton and Eli stretched the range of clothing styles in two directions: towards formality for Elton and informality for Eli. Elton's dress shirt and necktie present an image of the well-dressed man in Corvallis, Oregon; while Eli's capri pants, sandals and loose T-shirt are like the casual dress of men in his community of Kfar Adumim. For all six men, their appearance was one expression of their manhood.

Hegemonic masculinity was expressed most clearly by Eli, who considered one of his roles to be the children's protector. His community is located in a somewhat hostile political environment so he comes to work each day with a pistol concealed under his T-shirt. The slight threat of terrorist infiltration into the community provides an unmentioned background against which Eli constructs his male protector role.

Levien's masculinity comes to the fore in the yard where he playfully lifts and swings children around and participates in the children's sports activities. When the football flew out of the yard into the street, Levien rose to the occasion by retrieving the ball and kicking it into the playground with classic masculine bravado. Benny's fascination with movable tree stumps, planks and ropes on the playground showed a conventional masculine interest in creating movable outdoor play challenges for the children. His statement 'I've never been a woman' added to his apparently well-defined gender identity.

Elton's masculinity manifests itself through his formal attire of dress shirt and necktie, which define men in white collar jobs in his society. To this outfit he adds a lanyard with emblems of the local university football team, which broadcasts to colleagues, parents and the children a typically masculine love of sports. Although he does not engage in sports activities with the children on the playground, he talks men-talk about sports teams, and encourages the children to draw pictures and decorate the classroom with sports-related creations. In our interview, he frequently used the metaphor of father in describing his relationship with the children.

Both Leon and Reidar show a gentler side of the male image through their sensitive care of the young toddlers with whom they work. When I asked him how men differ from women in the role of caregiver, Reidar, like Benny, proudly responded that he had never been a woman so he could not tell me about such differences. By rejecting any understanding of how women feel and what they do, he clearly staked out his identity turf. Another marker of his masculinity is his description of his two professional role models from the past, both of whom were men. In contrast, Leon told me that he does not care what others think of him in terms of his gender identity – be it heterosexual or homosexual. While his positive feelings about himself as a man strengthen him to withstand whatever criticism comes his way, he tends to avoid such confrontations by not revealing his occupational choice to his male friends in the pub after football matches.

The teachers displayed a softer side too, each in his own way. This was a legitimate part of how they presented themselves in the work context. For example, Elton's necktie featured teddy bears, giving the masculine accoutrement an early childhood spin. Eli paid a great deal of attention to preparing composite posters of children's drawings in honour of two birthday celebrants, revealing his concern for aesthetics and bringing contrary evidence to his supervisor's claim that attention to the physical environment is not his strong suit. Benny's softer side appeared when he so sensitively dealt with the pain of a child who had bumped her head, and again when he graciously offered each child a selection from a beautifully arranged tray of fruit slices in honour of the Sabbath.

Leon's softer side came to the fore at nap time when he stroked the backs of his toddlers to help ease them into sleep. Both he and Reidar used the nappy change as an opportunity for quiet and relaxing banter with the toddlers so they would feel comfortable. Reidar's patience and intense focus on the needs of the child showed up in his response to a distressed child whose mother had just departed. For a full 15 minutes he carried the child around and comforted her.

Levien's softer side was the most difficult to discern. His choice of T-shirt touched humorously on this aspect of his self-image. Imprinted on the shirt was a large necklace with beads that formed the word 'pissing necklace', a reminder of the real pissing necklace that children were asked to wear around their neck when they left the classroom for the toilet. Levien seemed to be saying, 'Men can wear necklaces too, but our necklaces have a utilitarian purpose rather than making us look beautiful.' Thus the men's self-presentation and behaviour indicated the balance between dominant male features and hints towards a more gentle female presentation.

Touching, teaching and manhood

Physical contact is an integral part of work with young children, but for the men it poses a constant threat to their career as a childcare worker. Each teacher has come to grips with this challenge in his own way; yet their solutions are remarkably similar. A graded comparison of the six men according to their penchant for exhibiting outward signs of physical affection reveals some important features of their behaviour. Reidar comes first, as the caregiver who hugs, snuggles, lifts, cradles and holds the most. Following him is Levien who is quite comfortable with lifting children into his lap and swinging them around on the playground. While Montessori protocol dictates a polite handshake at the beginning and end of each day, Levien becomes much more affectionate during the day as he shifts to his own way of doing things. Eli also feels comfortable with small hugs and lightly holding children, and frequently brushing his hand through their hair. He is also a master at hugging children from the side, and he discourages lap sitting.

Leon's style of physical contact is functional. When a child needs to be held, he respectfully embraces her with empathy and care. He likes to lift children in his arms and carry them around if they need extra contact comfort. Benny is less physically demonstrative. I did not observe him initiating hugs or other forms of outward affection during my day in his class. When a child was distressed, he showed concern by lightly touching her forehead. Elton encourages what he calls proximity but he too does not offer hugs, kisses or other forms of outward affection.

While clear differences can be seen in their manner, they all find themselves the object of children's physical affection throughout the day. While such displays of fondness are not gender specific among the toddlers, in the kindergarten classes it is usually the girls who wrap their arms around their teacher, or dance around him while hanging on, as I observed in both Levien's and Elton's classrooms.

With each teacher I raised the issue of concerns over possible accusations related to touching. Although Leon and Reidar had no qualms about changing children's nappies in privacy, three of the kindergarten teachers, Eli, Levien and Benny, all said that they avoid helping children in the toilets when no other adults are present. If it is required, they will find a female staff member to do it, or make sure the door is open so they can be seen by others. The level of the teachers' concerns regarding physical contact was found to be related to their status in the school and community.

The most cautious teacher was Benny, the teacher with the least seniority of the six in his current job. Having worked at the synagogue school for less than a year at the time of my visit, he exhibited extreme vigilance in terms of avoiding outwardly demonstrable affection. At the other extreme was Elton, lovingly called 'Mr K' by the children and their parents. A veteran of 27 years, he has no concerns about physical contact with children. His only boundaries are self-imposed and based on his own sensibilities. Eli spoke of his respected place in the community and of the complete backing that parents grant him so he too hugs children without worries. Similarly, Levien has achieved total support from the parents and school administration and seemed unaware of any prohibitions about touching that might be found in the school policy. For all the men, touching in some form or another was a crucial component of their interactions with the children. Leon summed up the dilemma that addresses the professional lives of all six teachers and caregivers: 'As a male I have to be partly aware all the time that my interactions with the children cannot be misconstrued. But to be over-concerned would make proper interaction impossible.'

Their supervisors were all keenly aware of the inherent problems of male ECEC workers making physical contact with children. The most liberal attitudes were expressed by Ziona and Oivind, both of whom firmly support the need for teachers and caregivers to provide the physical contact the children require. Ziona, Eli's state inspector, places no limitations on touching, telling me: 'I believe that children deserve and need warmth and love and physical contact. It doesn't matter who the significant adult is (male or female) who works with the child.' Oivind outwardly encourages appropriate physical contact: 'I want them to touch the children. If they don't the children just die.'

Eva expressed the Montessori school's open policy, which permits physical contact with children, including lap sitting. The liberal attitudes that I found in Israel and Norway differed from those in the United States and England, where there are serious fears about teachers being accused of paedophilia and facing lawsuits (Carlson, 2006; Johnson, 1997). Denise therefore cautions her teachers, both male and female, against touching. She finds that male teachers are hyper-aware of these issues, and always make sure that they are never alone in a classroom with just one child. If such an occasion were to arise, they would always leave the door of the room open. Lorraine insisted that all her staff undergo training to learn appropriate forms of touch that will not leave the teacher vulnerable to accusations.

However Eric, the chairman of the board of Benny's private kindergarten in Basel, insisted that in order to achieve equal treatment of both genders he would not impose extra strictures on a male teacher. When viewed as a whole, the positions of the supervisors seem removed from the behaviour of the teachers and caregivers, who are generally not mindful of the attitudes of those in authority over them. Only Leon shows he is keenly aware of the well-articulated policies of the nursery and has undergone specific training about them.

When considering the impact of the touch issue on these teachers, we can say that their commitment to their careers with young children has served overall as a kind of immunity to the fear of possible accusation. For the most part, these men have carved out their career niche, and they feel quite comfortable there. Thus they may be said to exhibit a resilience that enables them to continue functioning in a way they deem appropriate for working with young children in spite of the looming threat of accusations.

Conclusions: Self-assurance within a cloud of suspicion

Whatever the social norms in which the six men function in their daily work, all operate under a cloud of suspicion. For some, like Eli and Reidar, the cloud may be off in the distance or even beyond the horizon. For others, such as Benny and Elton, the cloud looms almost overhead. When these men entered the profession of ECEC, they were largely unaware of this threat. Benny and Reidar were driven by a desire to find meaningful work, while Elton and Leon were looking for steady employment and a secure job. These motivations may have blinded them to the imposing challenges that lay ahead. They entered the profession believing they were doing the right thing for themselves at the time. Once they arrived in a training programme or on the job, they began to experience what it means to be a token minority, alone or with one or two other men in a female gender-defined territory. Again, circumstances differ. Isolated in his own separate building, Eli is largely unaware of his minority status, because he functions independently. Levien, on the other hand, sits in the teachers' room sharing coffee and stories with ten women and one man.

Outside influences serve to remind all of the men teachers and caregivers that they are swimming against the current – except for Reidar, whose waters are deeply egalitarian. All enjoy a high level of parental and supervisory support and the children with whom they work generate positive messages that their teachers are normal, responsible and responsive adults who can be loved and respected. It is when they move from their work world to their personal lives that they sometimes encounter social attitudes that remind them of their anomalous choice of profession.

Their awareness that they are doing 'women's work' poses a threat to their masculinity. This daily challenge, along with the close or distant cloud of suspicion, affects how they 'do gender' (Butler, cited in Jones, 2007). 'Doing gender' describes the presentation of the self in society to confirm one's gender identity and takes the form of outward signs, behaviour and attitudes. Each of these men openly confronts a gender duality that touches their personal and professional identity.

On the female side, these men engage in caring within the bounds of their culture. For example, Benny often avoids outward signs of physical affection out of caution, while at the same time engaging the children in physical and imaginative play and showing deep commitment to his work with them. My findings show that they choose caring behaviour that falls on the inclusive end of Vogt's continuum (2002), in acts that are acceptable for both men and women. Elton reminds us of this masculine disposition when he refers to his style as 'caring but not mothering'. Their performances of caring are strongly felt among the children.

Each educator has a unique manner of establishing his masculine identity that is recognized by his own society as described in the section on masculinity. Such signs and actions have been called 'performativity' of gender (Butler, cited in Jones, 2007: 190). Other masculine traits reveal themselves in their interactions with the children and in their expressed philosophies of education. They all encourage children to function independently and to act daringly. Beyond this, they support resilience by stressing the positive benefits of bearing pain and tolerating blood. These traits are not only styles of teaching but also statements about what it means in masculine terms to be a good learner.

Their investment in the children's learning seems to extend beyond gender identity to other teaching approaches that are considered best practice for both men and women. My findings show that all of these men diminish their own power and influence in order to make space for the children to act, think, grow and develop. By stepping aside, watching, internally applauding and sensitively mediating, they transfer to the children some of their power as ECEC caregiver and teacher. This self-effacement, considered by many to be a female trait, is coupled with leadership and charisma, both generally considered male traits. This combination involves a fluctuation between the role of active listening at individual level and proactive leadership at group level. Once again, this polarity of traits stresses the duality of their professional identity. They are compelled to express their masculinity alongside their loyalty to the caring traditions of the profession.

When viewed together, the cases presented and analysed in this book contribute a new perspective to the multiple discourses of men in ECEC (Nordberg, 2004). The discourse on the male role model is based on notions that children need men in their lives. My subjects and many of their supervisors appealed to this discourse in explaining the importance of their work. Their practice reveals a male role model that is hybridized, borrowing from Jones's (2007) notion of masculinity. The role model that these men exemplify is of a caring adult who likes to have fun and knows how to challenge and stimulate thinking. Only Elton refers to the fathering image; the others just want to be the teacher. The study builds up a composite picture of the male role model as is multifaceted.

The teachers and caregivers reflect the new man. They combine the gentle with the tough, emphasizing one side of the scale or the other. I suggest that the demands of the teacher or caregiver role, when combined with social pressures for conventional gender performativity, generate this new man paradigm as a suitable solution to the dilemma. Beyond the constructs of hybridized masculinity and the new man, a third alternative to the masculinity discourse raised by Nordberg (2004) is the undermining of gender dichotomy. These men unintentionally challenge the traditional distinctions between men and women not only in childcare but also on the broader playing field of gender identity. Through their successful functioning as caregivers and teachers of young children in six nations, they lend credence to the gender equality ideal. Each for his own reasons has entered the field of ECEC, survived and established a successful career. They are respected by family, colleagues and the parents of the children they teach because they are good at what they do, not because they are men. This established fact challenges, and perhaps undermines, gender dichotomy as a construct that hinders the provision of quality early education across the world. Their narratives suggest an alternative vision of what early education can be when both men and women passionately engage in the task.

This discussion of duality in personal and work identity of the six teachers leads us back to the issue of professionalism that I raised in the opening chapter: Can a different standard of professionalism for ECEC workers be applied to men from that applied to women? If teaching is equated with caring, as suggested by Noddings (2001), can a masculine brand of caring stretch the boundaries of ECEC professionalism? The subjects of my study demonstrate that professionalism in ECEC may look different for men and women. I have pointed out how the expressions of caring they have demonstrated may diverge from those of many of the women who work in the field. My findings suggest a new definition of professionalism in ECEC that aligns with the exigencies of men's lives in the nursery and kindergarten room, particularly as it relates to the constant scrutiny they endure. In negotiating the conflicting demands of caution on one hand and caring on the other, they have arrived at solutions that illustrate a valid professionalism that may be appropriate for other men in ECEC in other places and other times. The dilemma of professionalism versus caring could profitably be added to Nordberg's list of discourses regarding men in ECEC.

Connell (2005) has paved the way for considering multiple masculinities and Vogt (2002) has demonstrated multiple modes of caring. In these pages I have applied their paradigms to the variations of men's practice in ECEC from society to society. The various spectrums overlap and cross-pollinate, creating a rich understanding of what it means for men to teach and provide care to young children in group settings within a social context. While Gilligan (1995) and her followers claim the relational nature of women's outlooks, attitudes and actions, the men in the six different ECEC cultural contexts demonstrate that men, too, can define their work as relational and at the same time be 'real men' (Sargent, 2001). An example of the blend of the male and female modes can be found in these men's emphasizing children's independent functioning. Gilligan claims that the patriarchal mode is characterized by autonomy. The subjects in my study, while focusing on the relational, also encourage independence, which is closely connected to autonomy. This combination illustrates how men in ECEC cross boundaries of gendered dispositions when they choose to work in a profession defined by society as women's work.

An important factor that we see surfacing through the stories of the men in this study is their resilience as men and as ECEC caregivers and teachers. Against the backdrop of challenged masculinity, each has found his own way to feel comfortable as a man, and to present his own masculinity positively to those around him. Despite the cloud of suspicion looming somewhere in the distance, they continue to show warmth and concern for the children, and to find ways of physical contact that work for their own context. Their capacity to embrace outward signs of traditional male behaviour coexists with their ability to exhibit sincere caring. Their solution to the dilemmas raised by crossing the gender boundary is a mark of their strength and resilience and perhaps key to their successful adjustment to their anomalous career choice.

These men are all veterans in their work; they have chosen to remain in the classroom because they know that this is where they belong (Watson and Woods, 2011). Their self-assurance is well founded in their strong beliefs about the importance of their work and their own efficacy and successful practice. They have sought and built support networks that enable them to function proudly. Just as they encourage resilience in the children, so they achieve resilience for themselves. It may be that men who are attracted to ECEC are a special breed, characterized by their self-confidence and resilience. This claim may be supported by Sinclair and Carlsson's (2013) work on adolescents' gender identity and their occupational preferences. Those who experience a threat to their gender identity tend to have stereotypical preferences whereas these men's non-stereotypical occupational choice may indicate a strong gender identity, one that is nuanced by flexibility in their definition of gender roles.

Examination of male dropouts in the profession may offer an alternative explanation. Do those who survive exhibit self-confidence and resilience in distinction to those who drop out? A comparison of men who have remained in the profession with those who have dropped out would be fertile ground for further research. Writing this book has afforded me insight into my own journey as a man in early childhood education and has helped me appreciate my own resilience in surviving and thriving in the profession.

Breaking through stereotypes has challenged educators for many years. The growing presence of men in ECEC presents an opportunity to re-examine socially prescribed dictates about the capabilities of men, the unfounded accusations of the dangers of bringing them into the caregiving role, and the many positive benefits they offer to the education and care of young children. Further anthropological research is needed that would present a fine-grained analysis of gender roles in various societies as they relate to occupational gender anomaly, specifically as expressed by men in ECEC.

By focusing on men in these roles, this study has contributed to our understanding of differences and commonalities that can be found in their practice across cultures. Hopefully parents and policymakers alike will come to appreciate the contributions of such men to the care and education of young children, and will redouble their efforts to increase men's participation in the ECEC workforce. Initiatives to invite more men to enter the profession need to be accompanied by a broader atmosphere of tolerance and appreciation of the multiple masculinities and particular styles of caring that they bring to their work.

Appendix 1: Demographic data on the six teachers

name of teacher / characteristic	Benny	Elton	Levien	Eli	Leon	Reidar
Country	Switzerland	United States	The Netherlands	Israel	England	Norway
Age when began teaching	27	23	25	28	28	20
Age at time of interview	39	50	30	38	40	31
Years working in ECEC	12	27	5	10	12	11
Position	Kindergarten teacher	Kindergarten teacher	Kindergarten teacher	Kindergarten teacher	Nursery caregiver	Pedagogic leader (head teacher)
Family status	Married	Divorced + children	Single	Married + children	Single	Single
Background / training	Church youth work + 2 years teacher training certificate	BA in K-8 MEd Curriculum	BA in K-8, Montessori track	BEd in ECEC, MA Informal Education	Nursery caregiver training 2 years, NVQ level 3 course	BA in ECEC
Job description	Responsible for secular programme in a Jewish school, team-teaches at certain times	Teacher, self-contained class	Teacher, self-contained class	Teacher, self-contained class	Team-teaches with shared responsibility	Team leader
Supervisor	Board of the private school	School principal	School manager	State inspector	Day care centre director	Day care centre director

Appendix 2: Prompt for interviews with teachers

Introduction

I explained to you in my letter that I'm very interested in men kindergarten teachers. I myself was a kindergarten teacher for 16 years. In addition to teaching kindergarten, I also taught 2-year-olds, 3-year-olds, 4-year-olds and 5-year-olds. I am interested in learning about men who choose this profession and wish to talk to male kindergarten teachers in different countries around the world. I want to understand how the men in this profession see themselves and how they understand what they are doing in terms of the culture. Every country has its own culture and I am interested in learning if the phenomenon of men working in kindergartens is understood differently in different societies. That's why I asked to speak with you. My ultimate goal is to write a book in which each chapter is about one teacher. If you permit me, I will write a chapter about you. The way it works is that after I talk to you I will send you the transcript of our interview and ask your opinion about what I have written. It's important to me for you to look at it, and tell me 'That's what I said', or 'That's not what I said'. It's important for me to have material that is accurate. You get another chance to look at the material about you when I complete the chapter. I will send it to you and I will ask your permission to publish it. At any point you can say no, and then we will shake hands, and I will find another teacher. So you are in control of anything I do with this material about you.

Teacher and caregiver interview prompts:

1. Could you tell me about how you came to the profession of nursery caregiver/kindergarten teacher? What led you to this decision?

2. (If he speaks about training, then ask ...) Can you tell me about your experience as being a male minority among a majority of women in the training programme?

3. When you think of your work as a nursery caregiver/kindergarten teacher, which experiences are most important to you?

4. Does being a man make a difference to your contribution to the children here in the nursery/kindergarten?

5. What does a man do in the nursery/kindergarten class that differs from what a woman does?

6. Can you relate to me some of the things you have heard about the employment of men in early childhood education?

7. What would you say about the phenomenon of parents being sceptical of male nursery teachers because of paedophilia?

8. Is this an issue for male nursery teachers in your country? Does it cause problems? Do you think it affects a man's decision to enter the profession?

9. Does a man in the nursery/kindergarten class have to take precautions against suspicion?

10. Can you tell me about the reactions and responses of those with whom you work (parents, co-workers, supervisors) which you feel are related to you being a man?

11. Where do you see yourself ten years from now?

Appendix 3: Supervisor interview prompts

The introduction is similar to that used for the teachers.

1. Could you help me understand your role as director of the day care centre/manager of the school? Do you have hiring authority?

2. Have you had men on your staff in the past?

3. Could you tell me about your decision to hire a man on the staff? What led you to this decision?

4. In your opinion what do men bring to caregiving/teaching that may be different from women?

5. How do parents respond to the men on the staff?

6. How do the men caregivers/teachers get along with women on the staff? Can you tell me about the interaction?

7. Are there any issues for you about having a man teaching in the day care centre/school?

8. Have you ever had parents ask about having a man on the staff? Have parents shown concern?

9. In your experience, do your male caregivers/teachers work differently with the children? Is there something they do differently than women? To what extent do they fill the need for a male role model for a child from a single-parent family? Does it really work? Does it really matter?

10. Are there limits to how men are able to relate to the children physically?

11. Do you personally do anything to recruit men when you have a job opening?

12. In your experience with male caregivers/teachers, how do you see their trajectory? Do they tend to stay in the same job in the classroom? Do they tend to move up into administration? What happens to male teachers over the years?

13. Can you tell me about men in ECEC in your country?

Appendix 4: Early childhood groupings in different countries

Age \ Country	Switzerland (German-speaking)	United States	The Netherlands	Israel	England	Norway
0	Day care *Kinderkrippe*	Day care	Day care *kinderdagverblijf* crèche	Day care *maon*	Nursery	Kindergarten *barnehage kindergarten*
1	Day care *Kinderkrippe*	Day care	Day care *kinderdagverblijf* crèche	Day care *maon*	Nursery	Kindergarten *barnehage kindergarten*
2	Day care *Kinderkrippe*	Day care	Day care *kinderdagverblijf* crèche or play groups *peuterspeelzaal* or VVE *(voor- en vroegschoolse educatie)*	Day care *maon*	Preschool	Kindergarten *barnehage kindergarten*
3	Day care *Kinderkrippe*	Preschool	Day care *kinderdagverblijf* crèche or play groups *peuterspeelzaal* or VVE *(voor- en vroegschoolse educatie)* or preschool *(voorschool)*	Pre-kindergarten age 3 *gan trom trom hova*	Preschool	Kindergarten *barnehage kindergarten*
4	Kindergarten *Kindergarten*	Preschool	Primary school grade 1 or VVE *(voor- en vroegschoolse educatie)* or preschool *(voorschool)*	Pre-kindergarten age 4 *gan trom hova*	Preschool	Kindergarten *barnehage kindergarten*

Appendix 4: Early childhood groupings in different countries

Country Age	Switzerland (German-speaking)	United States	The Netherlands	Israel	England	Norway
5	Kindergarten *Kindergarten*	Kindergarten	Primary school grade 2 or VVE *(voor- en vroegschoolse educatie)* or preschool *(voorschool)*	Kindergarten *gan hova*	Reception class	Kindergarten *barnehage kindergarten*
6	Primary school grade 1 *Primarschule*	Elementary school grade 1	Primary school grade 3 or VVE *(voor- en vroegschoolse educatie)*	Primary school *beit sefer yesodi* grade 1	Key stage 1 primary school	Grade 1
7	Primary school grade 2 *Primarschule*	Elementary school grade 2	Primary school grade 4	Primary school *beit sefer yesodi* grade 2	Key stage 2 primary school	Grade 2
8	Primary school grade 1 *Primarschule*	Elementary school grade 3	Primary school grade 5	Primary school *beit sefer yesodi* grade 3	Year 3 primary school	Grade 3

References

Achterberg, P. and Houtman, D. (2009) 'Ideologically illogical? Why do the lower-educated Dutch display so little value coherence?'. *Social Forces*, 87 (3), 1649–70.

Acker, S. (1995) 'Carry and caring: The work of women teachers'. *British Journal of Sociology of Education*, 16 (1), 21–36.

Alkobi, O. (2008) 'Hatzad hanashi: Nashot avrechim tzioniyut-datiot' [From the woman's side: The wives of national religious yeshiva students], *Hagut B'hinuch Hayehudi*, 8, 87–106. (Hebrew).

Amar Levy, G. (2013) 'Zehut gavrit bekerev bogrei hahinuch hamamlachi-hadati' [Masculine identity among graduates of the religious schools], *Deot*, 59, 16–19. (Hebrew).

Andrews, M., Squire, C. and Tamboukou, M. (2008) *Doing Narrative Research*. Los Angeles: Sage.

Anliak, S. and Şahin Beyazkurk, D. (2008) 'Career perspectives of male students in early childhood education'. *Educational Studies*, 34 (4), 309–17.

Askland, L. (in press) 'Male kindergarten teacher assistants' perceptions of caring practice: Moving away from the misery rationale to build gender equality in childcare education'. In *Proceedings of the Conference on Engaging Men in Building Gender Equality*, Conference held at the University of Wollongong, Wollongong, Australia, November 2012.

Bieri Buschor, C., Berweger, S., Keck Frei, A. and Kappler, C. (2012) *'Geschlechts(un-)typische' Studienwahl: Weshalb Frauen Ingenieurwissenschaften studieren und Männer Primarlehrer werden*. Zürich: Pädagogische Hochschule. Online. www.phzh.ch/dotnetscripts/MAPortrait_Data/161973/9/Projektbericht_GUNST_Geschlechtsuntypische_Studienwahl_2012.pdf (accessed January 2014).

Bjornholt, M. (2009) 'Norwegian work-sharing couples project 30 years later: Revisiting an experimental research project for gender equality in the family'. *Equal Opportunities International*, 28 (4), 304–23.

Brind, R., Norden, O., McGinigal, S., Garnett, E. and Oseman, D. (2011) *Childcare and Early Years Providers Survey 2010*. London: Department for Education. Online. https://www.gov.uk/government/uploads/system/uploads/attachment_data/file/182041/OSR17-2011-Main_research_report.pdf (accessed January 2014).

Bryson, V. (2003) *Feminist Political Theory: An introduction*. New York: Palgrave Macmillan.

Cameron, C. (2001) 'Promise or problem? A review of the literature on men working in early childhood services'. *Gender, Work and Organizations*, 8 (4), 430–53.

— (2006) 'Men in the nursery revisited: Issues of male workers and professionalism'. *Contemporary Issues in Early Childhood*, 7 (1), 68–79.

Carlson, F.M. (2006), *Essential Touch: Meeting the needs of young children*. Washington DC: NAEYC.

CBS (Central Bureau of Statistics) (2004) *Teaching staff in pre-primary, primary and post-primary education, by level of education, sex, age, origin\religion and employment characteristics*. Online. www.cbs.gov.il/www/publications/education/kohot_oraa/year_koah3.pdf (accessed January 2014).

Connell, R.W. (2002) *Gender*. 2nd ed. Cambridge: Polity Press.

— (2005) *Masculinities*. 2nd ed. Berkeley: University of California Press.

Cooney, H.M. and Bittner, M.T. (2001) 'Men in early childhood education: Their emergent issues'. *Early Childhood Education Journal*, 29 (2), 77–82.

Coulter, R.P. (1993). 'Exploring men's experiences as elementary school teachers'. *Canadian Journal of Education*, 18 (4), 398–413.

Coulter, R.P. and Greig, C.J. (2008) 'The man question in teaching: A historical review'. *The Alberta Journal of Educational Research*, 18, 398–413.

Cremers, M., Höyng, S., Krabel, J. and Rohrmann, T. (2012) *Männer in Kitas*. Opladen: Barbara Budrich.

Day, C. and Kington, A. (2008) 'Identity, well-being and effectiveness: The emotional contexts of teaching'. *Pedagogy, Culture and Society*, 16 (1), 7–23.

Driessen, G. (2007) 'The feminization of primary education: Effects of teachers' sex on pupil achievement, attitudes and behaviour'. *Review of Education*, 54, 183–203.

Drudy, S. (2008) 'Gender balance/gender bias: The teaching profession and the impact of feminization'. *Gender and Education,* 20 (4), 309–23.

Duemmler, K., Dahinden, J. and Moret, J. (2010) 'Gender equality as "cultural stuff": Ethnic boundary work in a classroom in Switzerland', *Diversities*, 12 (1), 21–40.

Edlund, J. (2007) 'The work–family time squeeze: Conflicting demands of paid and unpaid work among working couples in 29 countries'. *International Journal of Comparative Sociology*, 48 (6), 451–80.

Eisenhauer, M.J. and Pratt, D. (2010) 'Capturing the image of a male preschool teacher'. *Young Children*, 65 (3), 12–16.

Ellingsaeter, A.L. and Leira, A. (2006) *Politicising Parenthood in Scandinavia*. Bristol: Polity Press.

Emilsen, K. (2012) 'Gender equality in Norwegian early childhood education and care institutions'. Paper presented at EECERA Conference, Porto, Portugal, August.

England, P. and Herbert, M.S. (1993) 'The pay of men in "Female" occupations: Is comparable worth only for women?'. In C.L. Williams (ed.), *Doing 'Women's Work': Men in nontraditional occupations*. London: Sage, 28–48.

Erikson, E.H. (1950) *Childhood and Society*. 1st ed. New York: Norton.

Farquhar, S.E. (2008) 'New Zealand men's participation in early years work'. *Early Child Development and Care*, 178 (7–8), 733–44.

Federal Office for Gender Equality (2008) *On the way to gender equality: Current situation and developments*. Neuchâtel: SFSO (Swiss Federal Statistical Office). Online. www.bfs.admin.ch/bfs/portal/en/index/news/publikationen. Document.114572.pdf (accessed January 2014).

Forrester, G. (2005) 'All in a day's work: Primary teachers "performing" and "caring"'. *Gender and Education*, 17 (3), 271–87.

Fougner Forde, B. and Hernes, M. (1988) 'Gender equality in Norway', *Canadian Woman Studies*, 9 (2), 27–30.

Francis, B., Skelton, C., Carrington, B., Hutchings, M., Read, B. and Hall, I. (2006) 'A perfect match? Pupils' and teachers' views of the impact of matching educators and learners by gender'. Paper presented at the British Educational Research Association Annual Conference, University of Warwick, September.

Friedman, S. (2010) 'Male voices in early childhood education and what they have to say'. *Young Children,* 65 (3), 41–5.

Furman, M. (1999) 'Army and war: Collective narratives of early childhood in contemporary Israel'. In E. Lomsky-Feder and E. Ben-Ari (eds), *The Military and Militarism in Israeli Society.* Albany: State University of New York Press, 141–68.

Gender in Norway (n.d.) 'Gender Equality'. Online. www.gender.no/Policies_tools/1078 (accessed 20 May 2014).

Gilligan, C. (1995) 'Hearing the difference: Theorizing connection'. *Hypatia,* 10 (2), 120–7.

Gladwell, M. (2008) *Outliers: The story of success,* New York: Little, Brown and Co.

Gonon, P., Haefeli, K., Heikkinen, A. and Ludwig, I. (eds) (2001) *Gender Perspectives on Vocational Education: Historical, cultural and policy aspects.* Pieterlen, Switzerland: Peter Lang AG, European Academic Publishers.

Hall, E.T. (1959) *The Silent Language.* New York: Doubleday.

Hansen, P. and Mulholland, J.A. (2005) 'Caring and elementary teaching: The concerns of male beginning teachers'. *Journal of Teacher Education,* 56 (2), 119–31.

Hirsch, A.A. (ed.) (2010) *Women and Men in Norway: What the figures say.* Statistisk sentralbyrå (SSB). Online. www.ssb.no/en/befolkning/artikler-og-publikasjoner/_attachment/39581?_ts=132b433a8c8 (accessed January 2014).

Hofstede, G.H. (2001) *Culture's Consequences: Comparing values, behaviours, institutions, and organizations across nations.* 2nd ed. Thousand Oaks, CA: Sage Publications.

Hong Li, J., Buchmann, M., Konig, M. and Saccbi, S. (1998) 'Patterns of mobility for women in female-dominated occupations: An event-history analysis of two birth cohorts of Swiss women'. *European Sociological Review,* 14 (1), 49–67.

Huri, R. (2013). 'Gever holech l'ibud: al gvarim v'ishivyon migdari' [Men get lost: On men and gender inequality]. *Deot,* 59, 38–41. (Hebrew).

Inglehart, R. and Norris, P. (2003) *Rising Tide: Gender equality and cultural change around the world.* Cambridge: Cambridge University Press.

Jacobs, J.A. (1993) 'Men in female-dominated fields, trends and turnover'. In Williams, C.L. (ed.) *Doing 'Women's Work': Men in nontraditional occupations.* London: Sage, 49–63.

Johannesen, N. and Hoel, A. (2010) 'Status of gender equality work in Norwegian kindergartens: New kindergartens in old tracks?'. Paper presented at EECERA Conference, Birmingham, UK, September. Online. www.koordination-maennerinkitas.de/uploads/media/EECERA__2010__Johannesen_Hoel_01.pdf (accessed January 2014).

Johnson B. (1963) 'On church and sect'. *American Sociological Review,* 28 (4), 539–49.

Johnson, R. (1997) 'The 'no touch' policy', in J. Tobin (ed.), *Making a Place for Pleasure in Early Childhood Education.* New Haven, CT: Yale University Press, 101–18.

Jones, D. (2007) 'Millennium man: Constructing identities of male teachers in early years contexts'. *Educational Review*, 59 (2), 179–94.

Kageyama, Y. (2006) 'Cuteness a hot-selling commodity in Japan'. *Washington Post*, 14 June. Online. www.washingtonpost.com/wp-dyn/content/article/2006/06/14/AR2006061401122.html (accessed January 2014).

Kaplan, D. (2006) *The Men We Loved: Male friendship and nationalism in Israeli culture*. New York: Berghahn Books.

King, J.R. (1998) *Uncommon Caring: Learning from men who teach young children*. New York: Teachers College Press.

Klein, U. (1999) '"Our best boys": The gendered nature of civil–military relations in Israel'. *Men and Masculinities*, 2 (1), 47–65.

— (2002) 'The gender perspective of civil–military relations in Israeli society'. *Current Sociology*, 50 (5), 669–86.

Koch, B. (2012) 'Strategies to increase the proportion of male child care workers – understanding processes of change'. Paper presented at EECERA Conference, Porto, Portugal, August.

Langfelt, T. (1987) *Barns sexualitet* [Children's sexuality]. Stockholm: Natur och Kultur. (Norwegian).

Marcon, R. (2012) 'The importance of balance in early childhood programs'. In S. Suggate and E. Reese (eds), *Contemporary Debates in Childhood Education and Development,* New York: Routledge, 159–68.

Martino, W. and Frank, B. (2006) 'The tyranny of surveillance: Male teachers and the policing of masculinities in single sex schools'. *Gender and Education,* 18 (1), 17–33.

Menka-Eide, A. (2012) '"Light years ahead": Norway's increasing recruitment of men into early childhood education'. Paper presented at EECERA Conference, Porto, Portugal, August.

Merriam-Webster Dictionary. Online. www.merriam-webster.com/dictionary/charisma (accessed January 2014).

Mirande, A. (2010) '"Macho": Contemporary conceptions'. In M.S. Kimmel and M.A. Messner (eds), *Men's Lives*. Boston: Allyn and Bacon, 26–36.

Moyles, J. (2001) 'Passion, paradox and professionalism in early years education'. *Early Years*, 21 (2), 81–95.

Nelson, B.G. (2002) *The Importance of Men Teachers: And reasons why there are so few*. Minneapolis, MN: MenTeach.

Nentwich, J. and Vogt, F. (2012) 'Dolls, building blocks and outdoor activity days: (Un)doing gender in the nursery'. Online. www.opsy.unisg.ch/Research/Gender+and+Diversity/UnDoing+gender+in+the+nursery.aspx (accessed January 2014).

Netzwerk Schulische Bubenarbeit (n.d.) Online. www.nwsb.ch

Nias, J. (1999) 'Primary teaching as a culture of care'. In J. Prosser (ed.), *School Culture*. London: Paul Chapman, 66–81.

Noddings, N. (2001) 'The caring teacher'. In V. Richardson (ed.), *Handbook of Research on Teaching*. 4th ed. Washington, DC: American Educational Research Association, 99–105.

— (2003) *Caring: A feminine approach to ethics and moral education*. 2nd ed. Berkeley: University of California Press.

— (2005) *The Challenge to Care in Schools: An alternative approach to education.* 2nd ed. New York: Teachers College Press.

Nordberg, M. (2004) 'Men in female occupations: Gender flexible models for gender transformations or hegemonic masculinity?' Paper presented at Konferensen Kvinnor Och Män På Den Nordiska Arbetsmarknaden Nordiskt (Women and men in the Nordic labour market), Reykjavík, November.

Norwegian Ministry of Children, Equality and Social Inclusion (2011) *Equality 2014 – The Norwegian government's gender equality action plan.* Oslo: Norwegian Ministry of Children, Equality and Social Inclusion. Online. www.regjeringen.no/upload/BLD/Action_plan_2014.pdf (accessed January 2014).

Nutbrown, C. (2012) *Foundations for Quality: The independent review of early education and childcare qualifications, final report.* London: Department for Education. Online. http://socialwelfare.bl.uk/subject-areas/services-activity/education-skills/departmentforeducation/foundations12.aspx (accessed January 2014).

OECD (2006) *Starting Strong II: Early childhood education and care policy.* Paris: OECD.

— (2012) *Education at a Glance 2012: OECD indicators.* OECD Publishing. Online. http://dx.doi.org/10.1787/eag-2012-en (accessed January 2014).

Olivier, J. (2011) '"In der Bank haben sie den Kopf geschüttelt" Andreas Terinieri, Kindergärtner'. *Schulblatt des Kantons Zürich*, 2, 38–9.

Osgood, J. (2006) 'Deconstructing professionalism in early childhood education: Resisting the regulatory gaze'. *Contemporary Issues in Early Childhood*, 7 (1), 5–14. Online. www.wwwords.co.uk/pdf/validate.asp?j=ciec&vol=7&issue=1&year=2006&article=2_Osgood_CIEC_7_1_web (accessed January 2014).

Oun, I. (2012) 'Work–family conflict in the Nordic countries: A comparative analysis'. *Journal of Comparative Family Studies*, 43 (2), 165–84.

Oyler, C., Jennings, G.T. and Lozada, P. (2001) 'Silenced gender: The construction of a male primary educator'. *Teaching and Teacher Education*, 17, 367–79.

Palgi, M. (2003) 'Gender equality in the kibbutz: From ideology to reality'. In K. Misra and M.S. Rich (eds), *Jewish Feminism in Israel: Some contemporary perspectives*. London: Brandeis University Press.

Peeters, J. (2003) 'Men in childcare: First results of a project in Flanders'. Paper presented at the European Conference on Men in Childcare, Ghent, November, 28.

— (2007) 'Including men in early childhood education: Insights from the European experience'. *NZ Research in Early Education*, 10. Online. http://stop4-7.be/files/janpeeters10.pdf (accessed January 2014)

— (2013) 'Towards a gender neutral interpretation of professionalism in early childhood education and care (ECEC)'. *Revista Española De Educación Comparada*, 21, 119–44. Online. www.uned.es/reec/pdfs/21-2013/05_peeters.pdf (accessed January 2014).

Perez, Y. (2009) 'Olamo shel haganan: kolam shel dvraim beisuke nashi muvhak', [The world of the male preschool teacher: The voice of men in a stereotypically female occupation]. MA thesis, The Schwartz Graduate Program in Early Childhood Studies, The Hebrew University. (Hebrew).

Praz, A.F. (2006) 'Ideologies, gender and school policy: A comparative study of two Swiss regions (1860–1930)'. *Paedagogica Historica*, 42 (3), 345–61.

Ray, R., Gornick, J.C. and Schmitt, J. (2008) *Parental Leave Policies in 21 Countries: Assessing generosity and gender equality*. Washington DC: Center for Economic and Policy Research. Online. http://tinyurl.com/pcrqltw (accessed January 2014).

Rivlin, Y. (2013) 'Gvarim hadashim, yehudim yeshanim' [New men, old Jews]. *Deot*, 59, 43–5. (Hebrew).

Rogers, S. (2012) 'Child care costs: How the UK compares with the world'. *The Guardian*, 21 May. Online. www.theguardian.com/news/datablog/2012/may/21/child-care-costs-compared-britain (accessed April 2014).

Rolfe, H. (2005) *Men in childcare*. Working Paper Series, 35. Manchester: Equal Opportunities Commission. Online. www.koordination-maennerinkitas.de/uploads/media/Rolfe-Heather.pdf (accessed January 2014).

Roulston, K. and Mills, M. (2000) 'Male teachers in feminized teaching areas: Marching the beat of the men's movement drums?'. *Oxford Review of Education*, 26 (3), 355–69.

Ryan, J. (2013) *Children in Poverty: Update 01–2013*. Greater London Authority Intelligence. Online. http://tinyurl.com/nev5fn5 (accessed January 2014).

Sargent, P. (2001) *Real Men or Real Teachers?* Harriman, TN: Men's Studies Press.

— (2004) 'Between a rock and a hard place: Men caught in the gender bind of early childhood education'. *The Journal of Men's Studies*, 12 (3), 173–92.

Schmitt, M. (1952) 'Research in northwest church history'. *Church History,* 21 (3), 259–66.

Schon, D. (1983) *The Reflective Practitioner: How professionals think in action*. London: Temple Smith.

Schwalbe, M., and Wolkomir, M. (2001) 'Interviewing men'. In J.F. Gubrium and J.A. Holstein (eds), *Handbook of Interview Research: Context and method*. Thousand Oaks, CA: Sage Publications, 203–20.

SFSO (Swiss Federal Statistical Office) (2004) *Educational Statistics*. Neuchâtel: SFSO. Online. www.bfs.admin.ch/bfs/portal/en/index/themen/15/22/lexi.Document.50496.pdf (accessed January 2014).

— (2012a) *Educational Statistics*. Neuchâtel: SFSO. Online. www.bfs.admin.ch/bfs/portal/en/index/themen/15/22/lexi.Document.171118.pdf (accessed January 2014).

— (2012b) *Education and Science: Panorama*. Neuchâtel: SFSO. Online. www.bfs.admin.ch/bfs/portal/en/index/themen/15/01/pan.Document.163202.pdf (accessed January 2014).

— (2013) 'Gender equality: Data, indicators'. Neuchâtel: SFSO. Online. www.bfs.admin.ch/bfs/portal/en/index/themen/20/05/blank/key/ueberblick.html (accessed January 2014).

Sheleg, Y. (2013) 'Ben Eisav leyaakov' [Between Jacob and Esau]. *Deot*, 59, 10–12. (Hebrew).

Sinclair, S. and Carlsson, R. (2013) 'What will I be when I grow up? The impact of gender identity threat on adolescents' occupational preferences'. *Journal of Adolescence*, 36 (3), 465–74.

Skelton, C. (2003) 'Male primary teachers and perceptions of masculinity'. *Educational Review,* 55 (2), 195–209.

Skjeie, H. and Teigen, M. (2005) 'Political constructions of gender equality: Travelling towards ... a gender balanced society?'. *NORA – Nordic Journal of Feminist and Gender Research*, 13 (3), 187–97.

Smedley, S. (2004) 'No man's land: Caring and male student primary teachers'. *Teachers and Teaching: Theory and Practice*, 6 (3), 259–77.

Statistisk sentralbyrå (SSB) (2010) 'Births and children, from generation to generation'. In Hirsch (2010).

Statistisk sentralbyrå (SSB) (2013) 'Immigration and emigration, 2012'. Online. www.ssb.no/en/befolkning/statistikker/innvutv/aar/2013-05-02 (accessed January 2014).

Steffens, M.C., and Wagner, C. (2004) 'Attitudes toward lesbians, gay men, bisexual women, and bisexual men in Germany'. *The Journal of Sex Research*, 41 (2), 137–49.

Stier, H. and Lewin-Epstein, N. (2007) 'Policy effects on the division of housework'. *Journal of Comparative Policy Analysis*, 9 (3), 235–59.

Strauss, A. and Corbin, J. (2008) *Basics of Qualitative Research: Techniques and procedures for developing grounded theory*. Los Angeles: Sage.

Sumsion, J. (2000) 'Negotiating otherness: A male early childhood educator's gender positioning'. *International Journal of Early Years Education*, 8 (2), 129–40.

Teigen, M. (2006) 'Die Norwegische Gender-Politik: Quoten und aktive Förderung' [Norwegian gender policy: Quotas and active promotion]. *WSI Mitteilungen*, 2006 (3), 138–43. (German).

Teigen, M. and Wängnerud, L. (2009) 'Tracing gender equality cultures: Elite perceptions of gender equality in Norway and Sweden'. *Politics and Gender*, 5 (1), 21–44.

Tuval, R., and Spector-Marzel, G. (2010), 'Mehkar narativi: teoria, yetzira vparshanut', [Narrative research: theory, creation, and interpretation]. Tel Aviv: Machon Mofet. (Hebrew).

Tzaban, H. (2012). 'Hachsharat gananot b'yisrael' [Training preschool teachers in Israel]. In A. Kimhi (ed.), *Hahinuch vkdam yesodi b'yisrael: hebetim irguniim v'demographiim* [Preschool education in Israel: Organizational and demographic perspectives]. Jerusalem: Taub Center for Social Policy Research in Israel, 127–54. (Hebrew).

Vogt, F. (2002) 'A caring teacher: Explorations into primary school teachers' professional identity and ethic of care'. *Gender and Education*, 14 (3), 251–64.

Watson, L.W. and Woods, C.S. (eds) (2011) *Go Where You Belong: Male teachers as cultural workers in the lives of children, families, and communities*. Rotterdam: Sense.

Webb-Dempsey, J., Bruce Wilson, B., Corbett, D. and Mordecai-Phillips, R. (1996) 'Understanding caring in context: Negotiating borders and barriers'. In D. Eaker-Rich and J. Van Galen (eds), *Caring in an unjust world: Negotiating borders and barriers in schools*. Albany, NY: SUNY Press, 85–109.

Williams, C.L. (1992) 'The glass escalator: Hidden advantages for men in the "female" professions'. *Social Problems*, 39 (3), 253–67.

Williams, L.S. and Villemez, W.J. (1993) 'Seekers and finders: Male entry and exit in female-dominated jobs'. In C.L. Williams (ed.), *Doing 'Women's Work': Men in nontraditional occupations*. London: Sage, 64–90.

Woltring, L. (2009) 'Working Forum on Men in Early Childhood Education'. World Forum Foundation. Online. www.worldforumfoundation.org/networking-grant (accessed May 2014).

— (2012) 'Get the good guys in and the wrong guys out: Prevention of abuse embedded in good quality management'. *Child Links*, 1, 15–19.

Wu, Y. (2010) 'More men becoming kindergarten teachers.' *China Daily*, 1 June. Online. http://usa.chinadaily.com.cn/2010-06/01/content_11019298.htm

Yamamoto, Y., Holloway, S.D. and Suzuki, S. (2006) 'Maternal involvement in preschool children's education in Japan: Relation to parenting beliefs and socioeconomic status'. *Early Childhood Research Quarterly*, 21 (3), 332–46.

Young, M. and Willmott, P. (1992) *Family and Kinship in East London*. Originally 1957. Berkeley: University of California Press.

Index